Embrace the Hit

by:

Courtney Spencer

Table of Contents

Acknowledgments

— ✦ —

I dedicate this book to my children. Through you, I have come to see even more clearly how precious the gospel of Jesus Christ truly is, especially when it becomes the foundation of a young testimony.

The influence of the Holy Ghost has guided and protected me in every circumstance, so long as I sought Him and welcomed Him in.

I am deeply grateful for my parents, family members, friends, and teachers who nurtured me in the teachings of my Savior. My hope is that this book will, in some small way, be a good influence on the rising generation in our family.

It is the record of my journey to find Jesus Christ, accept His gospel, take upon His name, and share my witness of the truthfulness of the Book of Mormon and the joy that comes from following the prophet.

Jesus Christ is the head of The Church of Jesus Christ of Latter-day Saints, and I will continue to follow Him. I also dedicate these words to the young women, young men, and young single adults.

Your choices and your story matter, both in this life and in the eternities. Embrace the joy, even when it tests everything within you. You are never alone.

For you:

Ada & Sterling and those to come.

Preface

—✦—

In the pages that follow, some stories involving friends and family have been adapted to protect their privacy. Names and specific descriptive details have been changed or omitted, and in some cases, experiences of multiple individuals have been woven into a single character. However, the essence of each experience remains true.

Introduction

— ✦ —

This book is written to shed light on the reality of personal opposition, drawing on my own experiences and the accounts of others who have shared their journeys with me. It serves as both a witness and a warning: the adversary, Satan, will never cease in his efforts to pull us away from Jesus Christ.

My hope is that as you read, the Spirit of the Holy Ghost will confirm to your heart that your Father in Heaven loves you deeply. You are not just another person in the world; you are His cherished son or daughter, an eternal being with divine potential. He longs to bless you abundantly and invites you to choose to become an instrument in His work.

The Most High God is aware of you specifically. He knows your struggles, your desires, and your heart. If you allow Him, He will reveal His hand in your trials and difficulties. Hardship, problems, and adversity are not meaningless; some are tailored to you for a divine purpose. They can teach, refine, and even bring peace and love beyond understanding, but only when you involve the Savior, Jesus Christ.

Turn to Him. Pray in His holy name to a loving Father in Heaven, and listen for the comfort and direction of the Holy Ghost. I know these small and simple steps lead toward our Celestial home. I have felt the healing and peace of my Redeemer. Truly, He is the Prince of Peace.

President Russell M. Nelson taught:

"Worldly identifiers will never give you a vision of who you can ultimately become. They will never affirm your divine DNA or your unlimited, divine potential."

He promised, "As you embrace these truths, our Heavenly Father will help you reach your ultimate goal of living eternally in His holy presence."

May these pages point you toward that truth and deepen your trust in the Savior who knows and loves you perfectly.

Chapter One

✦

When Your Faith Has Holes in It

"The Lord Does Not Require Perfect Faith for Us to Have Access to His Perfect Power. But He Does Ask Us to Believe. This Emphasizes That Faith Is Not About Achieving a Flawless State, But Rather a Choice to Believe and Act Despite Uncertainties." - President Russel M. Nelson

There's no shortage of things we're asked to endure in this life: sickness, unfairness, careless words, financial strain, loneliness, silence where we hoped for connection, being misjudged or misunderstood... and at times, even opposition from those who treat us like enemies.

"Enduring" was always an interesting word to me when I read it in 2 Nephi 31:15, "Yea, the words of my Beloved are true and faithful. He that endureth to the end, the same shall be saved."

Of all the things our Heavenly Father could have emphasized in that moment, He chose to stress endurance. Why?

Elder Neal A. Maxwell said, "First, because God has repeatedly said He would structure mortality to be a proving and testing experience (see Abraham 3:25; Mosiah 23:21)."

Every one of us, in some form or another, comes face to face with the very trials that test what we believe and who we trust.

Enduring doesn't just mean surviving. It means allowing the hard things to draw us nearer to Christ. To embrace them and use them. When we take His yoke upon us, even in our small and personal ways, we begin to learn of Him, not just about Him. And it's in that process, step by step, that we start to become like Him.

You can and should continue to educate yourself, not only when you feel uncertain about what to do, but also when you already know the right path and just haven't been able to accomplish it... yet. There are countless resources available to you, including trusted friends, family, mentors, and even strangers. The scriptures, along with living prophets and apostles, offer inspired direction. Libraries, online resources, and communities of knowledge place an entire ecosystem of truth and perspectives at your fingertips.

And yet, if you're anything like me, you may find yourself bypassing the searching, learning, pondering, and wrestling that uncover absolute truth. Why? Because of a "leech" I call instant gratification.

It clings tightly. You may feel its pull, too, that whisper that says, there's a quicker, easier fix. It promises relief with minimal effort. But like a flimsy sticker, the solution doesn't last. Sooner or later, it begins to peel, warp, or fall away, leaving the real problem untouched. Worse, this patch often masks the deeper issue, allowing it to grow, while you compensate in other ways. Over time, those compensations can harden into habits that are even harder to break.

Take sports, for example. Imagine trying to master a game without proper training, teaching yourself instead of seeking out a coach, a skilled player, or even consistent practice with others. You'd almost certainly develop poor form and incorrect techniques. Eventually, those shortcuts would cost you, perhaps even getting you called out by a referee and removed from the game, or worse, resulting in injury to yourself or another. The truth is, learning the foundational movements, rules, and strategies from the start sets you up for long-term success. So why do we so often slap on a "sticker-solution," even when we know the deeper investment will yield lasting results?

The same principle applies to something as simple as hunger. A snack may take the edge off, but it won't truly satisfy you. Worse, filling up on cake and doughnuts may trick you into feeling full, but it won't nourish you or sustain your energy. Soon after, you'll crash, your motivation, focus, and strength drained. The "sticker-solution" gave immediate satisfaction, but not the lasting fuel your body actually needed.

Understanding the difference between a "sticker-solution" and a real solution changes everything. It helps us recognize when we're reaching for a quick fix instead of addressing the root of the issue. It reminds us that while the easy patch may feel good in the moment, only the deeper, truer choice will sustain us, strengthen us, and set us up for growth.

Why do I call instant gratification a leech? Because it silently drains the will to apply real effort. And like a leech, you may not even notice it clinging to you. Over time, instant gratification can become a habit that offers no true benefit, only a false sense of relief.

So why do we condition ourselves to let this metaphorical parasite suck away our long-suffering and patience?

For a long time, I thought life would be unbearably dull if it followed a straight, predictable path, no bumps, no twists, no surprises. But then came seasons of life that felt like whirlwinds, and I found myself on my knees praying for that simple, steady boredom I once dismissed. That's human nature. Change is hard. But as the Prophet has reminded us, "The Lord loves effort." And what better test of effort than finding yourself wedged between a rock and a hard place?

I lived in that space for nearly ten years. During that time, I often reached for instant gratification. Sometimes it was my own choice, other times the choices of others left me broken and emotionally desolate. In that dark hole, I realized I had two options: remain in misery, or seek to understand why the Lord designed this life the way He did.

As I began to learn His ways, I was blessed with eyes to see and ears to hear how He could help me change. This book is about that process, how I began to metabolize trauma. In the thick of it, I often felt caught in what my father-in-law calls the "maybe so, maybe not" moments of life, quoting an old Chinese proverb. The truth is, we don't always know until later. But with reflection and the guidance of the Holy Ghost, we can rewire our perspective and recognize the Lord's hand in our lives, as well as in the people He places along our path, even when we are in the thick of it.

Too often, we wish for circumstances or opportunities to be easy, instead of embracing the divine traits that make us human: the ability to reason, to choose, and to labor diligently in pursuit of good. My husband's mission president once told us, "Blessed are the flexible for they will never be broken." I feel a responsibility to add my voice to the conversation about embracing all truth.

As John B. Dickson once taught:

"Life is not intended to be easy, but I promise those that labor faithfully in the service of their fellowmen, and with determination handle every challenge properly and under the influence of the Spirit, that they will be blessed with feelings of happiness which will permeate their whole souls. These...are blessings that mold and build us, and can never be taken away."

Difficulty does not mean you are on the wrong path. Trials are not punishments from the Lord, nor evidence that He has abandoned you. They are part of His design to help us grow to be more like Him.

We have to follow the example of Jesus Christ when it comes to our trials. He showed us how to pray when He said, "If it be possible, let this cup pass from me: nevertheless not as I will, but as thou wilt." That line teaches us how to trust. There will be times in our lives when we ask Heavenly Father to remove the burden, to soften the blow, and sometimes, the answer will be no.

Not because He doesn't love us, but because He does.

Sometimes, if the Lord stepped in the way we wanted Him to, it would undo everything we've been learning, stretching, and becoming up to that point. He sees the full picture. He knows what we need to go through to become who He created us to be.

Gethsemane and Calvary remind us that even the Savior wasn't spared from suffering, and yet He chose to trust the Father. We're asked to do the same: to kneel down, ask with faith, and then, if the answer is to walk through the trial, to do it with a willing heart.

The Lord will not cut short any trial that He has designed along with you for your benefit.

As George Q. Cannon taught:

"Knowledge...is righteous power."

Some lessons I have learned through trial and error. Others I have absorbed by simply reflecting on my Savior's attributes, meekness, sacrifice, patience, faithfulness, and humility. But one thing I know: enduring hardship with faith always brings a harvest of wisdom. As the Prophet Joseph Smith taught,

"We gain knowledge of eternal truths a little at a time; we can learn all things as fast as we are able to bear them."

Elder Neal A. Maxwell once gave a striking description, later expanded on by Elder Jeffrey R. Holland:

"One's life cannot be both faith-filled and stress-free. It simply will not work to glide naively through life, saying as we sip another glass of lemonade, 'Lord, give me all thy choicest virtues, but be certain not to give me grief, nor sorrow, nor pain, nor opposition. Please do not let anyone dislike me or betray me, and above all, do not ever let me feel forsaken by Thee or those I love. In fact, Lord, be careful to keep me from all the experiences that made Thee divine.

And then, when the rough sledding by everyone else is over, please let me come and dwell with Thee, where I can boast about how similar our strengths and our characters are as I float along on my cloud of comfortable Christianity."

The truth is clear: opposition is essential. Growth is impossible without it. That's why we need the gift of the Holy Ghost, to discern truth, to feel when it's time to shift direction, and to recognize God's invitations in our lives.

I think back to when I first tried out for the Winter Olympic sport of Skeleton at age twenty-six. It had been years since my college lacrosse days at Baylor University, and I felt wildly out of my depth. But I marvel at how the Lord placed the right people in my path, at exactly the right time, to extend an opportunity to me that led to choices I never imagined I would make.

I was working at a WeWork on 28th and Park Avenue when, on a day like any other, I decided I needed a brain break. A hot cup of something always gave me the motivation to power through the rest of my work. So, I wandered into the shared kitchen to make a cup of lemon ginger tea.

As I waited for the water to boil, a woman approached me. Without introducing herself, she looked me straight in the eye and said confidently, "You have the perfect body type for Skeleton."

I blinked, unsure if she was even talking to me. I glanced around the room, but her eyes stayed locked on mine. "What is Skeleton?" I asked.

Instead of answering, she countered with a question of her own: "What sport do you play?"

I told her about my background, thirteen years of gymnastics, followed by track, lacrosse, and cheerleading in high school, and most recently, collegiate lacrosse. "These days, I mostly run and do yoga," I added.

She nodded, then shared her own story. She had been a collegiate volleyball player who missed the competitive fire and community of athletics. While training for CrossFit, someone had once approached her, much like I was now being approached, and suggested she try bobsledding.

The conversation ended quickly, and I went back to my desk. But my mind couldn't let go. What was Skeleton?

When I returned to my desk, curiosity got the better of me. I Googled it and discovered skeleton is a Winter Olympic sport where athletes race face-first down an icy track, with their chin just inches from the ice, hitting speeds of 80–90 miles per hour, with no brakes.

And without overthinking, I signed up for a combine.

Before I share what came next, the steps that forever changed the course of my life, I want to pause on what I learned in that kitchen moment.

Breaks matter.

That day, I didn't need a week-long vacation at a spa. I simply needed to step away from my work, shift my perspective, and recharge. For me, a warm drink in a mug has become a gentle cue, reminding me that I can choose happiness. More often than not, as the soothing taste of chamomile, Guayusa, or mint tea touches my lips, I pause to reflect, to search for gratitude, and to notice the hand of the Lord in my life.

Choosing to be still and to seek happiness is, at its core, an act of faith.

The Prophet Joseph Smith once taught:

"Happiness is the object and design of our existence; and will be the end thereof, if we pursue the path that leads to it; and this path is virtue, uprightness, faithfulness, holiness, and keeping all the commandments of God."

Echoing this truth, President Russell M. Nelson shared in his 2016 message, Joy and Spiritual Survival:

"The joy we feel has little to do with the circumstances of our lives and everything to do with the focus of our lives."

Whatever it is for you, find it. Build it into your daily life. Sometimes that means physically stepping back; other times, it's being still in the middle of chaos. A prayer, some meditation, a walk, or even a hot cup of something, whatever helps jumpstart your mind to search, ponder, and pray with a heart full of gratitude. As I've discovered, "we walk in the direction we are facing." So if you find yourself spiraling downward with stress, fear, or anxiety, turn upward. Lift your face toward Him. Involve our Savior, Jesus Christ.

He may not take away the burden, but He will help you carry it.

And like a car, life doesn't stop unless you know how to apply the brakes. If you hit the accelerator instead, you may find yourself speeding into burnout without even realizing it. That's why prayer, journaling, and trusted conversations are so vital; they help us recognize when it's time to pause, reset, and refocus.

Breaks can be life-changing. They can shift your entire trajectory if you let the Savior be part of them.

My first Skeleton combine was at the Olympic Training Center in Lake Placid, NY. The drive up was breathtaking, snow-blanketed mountains under a bright cerulean sky. My nerves tangled with awe as I pulled in, wondering what I was about to face.

The test included a 45-meter sprint, a broad jump, and a 12-pound shot put throw. Some combines also tested Olympic lifts.

I felt wildly unprepared. That very morning, I'd scrambled through upstate New York to find track spikes, and the only pair I could get was a size too small. Meanwhile, other athletes arrived looking like professionals, in spandex layers, with Tiger Balm and extra spikes in hand. I was intimidated and out of place.

When the results were posted outside the cafeteria, I scanned the list. My eyes trailed all the way to the bottom.

Courtney Webb.

Dead last.

Humiliation washed over me. My shoulders slumped as I replayed every doubt in my mind: Who did I think I was? Showing up for a sport I'd never even heard of until days ago? Learning an Olympic sport in my late twenties? This was a mistake.

I sat alone in the cafeteria, staring at my mashed potatoes and secretly praying, asking the Lord why He had led me here only to leave me feeling like a failure.

And then the young woman from WeWork appeared.

Wide-eyed and grinning, she bent down to meet my lowered gaze and practically shouted, "NO WAY! YOU ACTUALLY SHOWED UP!" She said it twice, her face enthusiastic with excitement.

Before I knew it, she was calling out to other athletes across the room, telling them how she'd met me randomly in New York and how amazed she was that I'd really come.

They invited me over to their table to finish my meal. One by one, they started encouraging me: "You did awesome! The hardest part is showing up." Another athlete held out his hand for a high-five.

Moments later, I was sitting at a table with seven other Olympic athletes and hopefuls, listening to their stories of injuries, financial struggles, setbacks, and resilience. Each had overcome obstacles just to be there.

The young women from the WeWork then took me to the push track outside, where I got my first real introduction to Skeleton technique. I wasn't great, but it didn't matter. My shame melted away, replaced by the determination to keep trying.

I showed up humbled and left motivated.

I showed up unprepared and left inspired.

I showed up alone and left supported.

From those athletes, I learned that true greatness isn't about flawless performance. It's about showing up, humbled, willing, and ready to learn. It's not always about the outcome you hoped for; it's about how you choose to respond to what actually unfolded.

As Stephen W. Owen taught in General Conference:

"The world teaches that leaders must be mighty; the Lord teaches that they must be meek. Worldly leaders gain power and influence through their talent, skill, and wealth. Christlike leaders gain power and influence 'by persuasion, by long-suffering, by gentleness and meekness, and by love unfeigned.'"

The best leaders are first willing followers. As I sat with these incredibly talented individuals, my respect for them grew, not just because of their skill but because of how they treated the people around them. These athletes didn't openly share whether they believed in Jesus Christ, but they radiated Christ like love in the way they showed up for others.

So when I saw new faces at later combines, I made a point to encourage them, just as my friend from WeWork and others had done for me. I'd listen to their sacrifices, share what I'd learned, and remind them that showing up was already a victory.

In God's eyes, the greatest leaders have always been the greatest followers.

One of the most important qualities I took away from my experiences with elite athletes was a deceptively simple one: show up and support others in positive ways.

That principle stuck with me. When you find yourself dreading a ward activity or hesitating to say hello to someone sitting alone, remember, your presence matters not just to those around you, but to the Lord. He wants us gathered with those who love Him. He wants us to seek out the one and invite them into the fold. And I say this as someone who can struggle with introversion. We show up not to be seen, but to help others feel seen. And that makes all the difference.

There are going to be days when the voices come:

"I'm not good enough to be here."

"I'm not ready."

"I don't even want to be here right now."

But here's the truth: your present circumstances are not an accident. They are the sum of every step you've taken, every decision that has shaped you into who you are right now. Even when it feels like you don't belong, you are exactly where you need to be.

So my advice is this: show up.

Show up when it's uncomfortable. Show up when you feel unqualified. Show up when you'd rather hide. You have a choice in this position. Bring with you a willingness to learn and the humility to grow, and you'll be surprised at how God magnifies your efforts.

In Skeleton, I had mentors who transformed the way I saw myself, not just as an athlete, but as a person. They lifted me when I stumbled, reminded me that gratitude is possible even in failure, and gave me the courage to view mistakes not as endings, but as beginnings.

This was my takeaway from doing multiple combines: trying new things builds resilience. Failure is not the enemy; it's the first stepping stone. Vulnerability, I came to realize, is gold. It reveals what's really under the hood, what you have to work with, and accountability is the fuel that helps you move closer to your potential. And if you're willing to see potential in others, you must also be willing to hold them accountable.

After my very first combine, I flew back to New York humbled and determined. I knew I wasn't ready, so I hired a coach to help me train for the next two. Looking back, I can see that my approach mirrored how I had come to learn about the gospel of Jesus Christ.

At first, I had wanted to rely on familiar voices, friends who meant well but knew nothing of the Book of Mormon. But if I truly wanted to know, I had to seek out credible sources. I began with members who had testimonies of the Book of Mormon. I studied the chapters for myself. I prayed, sometimes desperately, to know if the book was true. For months, I filled journals with my questions and the impressions I received. Slowly, steadily, I gained a confirmation so strong and undeniable that it anchored me. I knew the Book of Mormon was the most correct book on earth.

Training for the combines was no different. I went to experts, coaches, nutritionists, and fitness professionals whom I had met during my years as a fitness journalist in New York. I studied what to eat, how to recover, and how to prepare my body for the demands of Skeleton.

And here's what I've learned, not just in sports but in every corner of life: the more you do, the more God gives you. The more effort you put into knowing Him, the clearer His mysteries become. The more time and energy you dedicate to something that is of good report, virtuous, lovely, or praiseworthy, He magnifies it, if you include Him and seek His will in the process.

I improved with each combine. By the third, a skeleton coach pulled me aside and suggested I spend November and December training on the Park City track. That suggestion landed like a thunderclap.

Leaving New York for two months wasn't just inconvenient; it felt impossible. I'd have to give up my job, find a place to live, secure a car, and somehow get my hands on Skeleton equipment, which, for the record, isn't exactly stocked at Dick's Sporting Goods. Type "Skeleton" into a search bar, and you're more likely to find Halloween decorations than actual gear.

The idea felt outrageous. Wild, even. But I knew one thing with absolute certainty: I had been paying my tithing. And with that obedience came a promise that God would bless me. Maybe not in the way I imagined, but in the way I needed. He would provide. And so I stepped forward in faith.

Chapter Two

— ✦ —

What to Do with Persistence?

"One of The Greatest Weaknesses in Most of Us Is Our Lack of Faith in Ourselves. One of Our Common Failings Is to Depreciate Our Tremendous Worth." – Tom L. Perry

I didn't know it then, but persistence, true persistence, would become the theme of my story.

Persistence is more than just stubbornness or grit. It's about continually choosing to act in faith, even when you don't yet see the outcome. As David A. Bednar, once said:

"What is faith in Jesus Christ? It is the principle of action, followed by power. The sequence is first, we act in accordance with the teachings of the Savior, then we are blessed with His power."

That sequence would define my journey.

I was living in Manhattan when I met a guy on a dating app. On our third date, he casually mentioned that he was "Mormon." I fixed him with a bewildered gaze. I had no idea what that meant. Until that moment, I had never heard of the Book of Mormon, never seen a Temple, never met a missionary.

I had grown up Lutheran, baptized as an infant, educated in a Lutheran school, and later attended a Baptist university. My mom was Lutheran, my dad Baptist. I figured I had a solid grasp of Christianity. So, imagine my surprise when, on that third date, I learned about an entire denomination of Jesus Christ that I had never even heard of. Naturally, I had questions.

Those questions turned into long conversations. He explained what it meant to be a member of The Church of Jesus Christ of Latter-day Saints, and I listened, curious, yet guarded. Soon, I found myself sitting beside him at church services, still telling him, 'I'm not going to be baptized,' but unable to resist learning more.

Now, years later, as a member of the Church, I see it differently. I believe the Lord doesn't present truths to us until we are ready to receive them.

Back when I lived in Houston, for example, I used to drive a route that passed right in front of the Houston Temple. If you've ever seen a Temple, you know it's impossible to miss, large, bright, and meticulously cared for. And yet, I never noticed it. Not once.

Today, when I go back and drive that same road, I can't help but wonder: How could I not have seen it?

The answer, I've come to realize, is simple: I wasn't ready. My eyes weren't open in that season of my life.

Sister Michelle D. Craig expressed it beautifully:

"As I pray for the Lord to open my eyes to see things I might not normally see, I often ask myself two questions: 'What am I doing that I should stop doing?' and 'What am I not doing that I should start doing?'"

Her words mirror my own experience. At that time, there were many things I needed to stop, or start, before I would ever notice the Temple offered up to me.

Later in my life, a woman once told me, "You know what you are? You are a seeker."

When she said it, I knew she was right. I had always carried a hunger to learn, to understand, to find out what God wanted me to receive. Even before I chose to be baptized, I can see now how that trait was quietly unfolding.

When that young man first told me about a denomination of Jesus Christ I had never even heard of, what did I do? I started attending church with him. And then, still not knowing it was the restored Church of Jesus Christ, I invited him to my church as well. For months, we found ourselves in pews for five or six hours every Sunday, one service after another.

I devoured everything I was learning, though with hesitation. I told him more than once, "I'm not going to be baptized, but I find what's being taught interesting. And I believe a good portion of it."

He gave me a copy of the Book of Mormon. I thanked him, then promptly slid it onto my bookshelf, where it sat untouched.

I even became curious enough about Temples that one day I asked him, "Do you want to get married, or sealed, in the Temple?"

Without a pause, he answered, "Yes."

I looked him straight in the eye and said, "Then why are you dating me?"

The silence that followed was brief but heavy. Not long after, we decided to part ways.

That summer, a friend invited me to stay with her in Watermill, New York, to help launch her tennis company. I agreed and began packing for a few weeks on the eastern end of Long Island.

As I slid clothes into a suitcase, I thought, I'll need a beach read. My eyes scanned a bookshelf crowded with self-help books and titles friends had recommended. That's when I saw it: a small navy blue book.

The Book of Mormon.

I had a rule: if a good friend recommended a book, I would read it. If I disliked it, I'd quietly donate it and never mention it again. If I liked it, I'd keep it and share it with others.

So there it was, the little blue book, waiting patiently for me to finally pick it up.

Curious, I asked myself, "What exactly is the Book of Mormon?" I reached for it and read the cover:

"Another Testament of Jesus Christ."

I froze. I had always assumed it was Joseph Smith's journal. I was wrong.

Before I knew it, the book was in my bag as I boarded the Hampton Jitney, the bus that would take me east, since I had no car in Manhattan.

That first night in Watermill, after a long day helping my friend, I settled into my night time routine. And then a thought, so faint it could have been missed, whispered into my mind:

You should pray to know if the Book of Mormon is true. And then read it.

I remembered hearing that suggestion in church, though I'd brushed it off at the time. But now, in the quiet of my room, it pressed gently on my heart.

I pulled out my journal and pen, because I can't read without them, and then knelt.

For the first time, I prayed the way I had learned in The Church of Jesus Christ of Latter-day Saints: beginning with "Dear Heavenly Father" and ending with "In the name of Jesus Christ."

This simple way of praying resonated deeply with me. Growing up, the Trinity had been described to me as "three in one," but I had always quietly believed they were three distinct beings with a united purpose. Now, the words I had learned in the Latter-day Saint Church gave voice to what I had always felt.

After praying, I sat down with my pen poised to underline everything I disagreed with. My determination was clear: I'll show them.

But that isn't what happened.

As I began reading 1 Nephi, something stirred inside me. By verse 12, I read,

"And it came to pass that as he read, he was filled with the Spirit of the Lord."

Instead of marking what I rejected, I found myself underlining what I knew to be true. Page after page, the words sank into my heart like light finding cracks in a closed curtain.

Some truths were familiar, affirming things I had always believed to be true. Others were brand new, yet they felt instantly right, as if I had known them all along.

I couldn't stop reading. I wanted more, needed more. Questions I had carried for years began to unravel with answers so simple and clear that I wondered why I hadn't seen them before.

That first night, I read until my eyes grew heavy. I fell asleep with the book beside me. In the morning, I woke eager to read again. This became my rhythm: scripture at night, scripture in the morning, whenever I could squeeze it in.

By the time I boarded the bus back to Manhattan, I knew I couldn't ignore what was happening. I texted the sister missionaries whose number I still had:

"I want to meet when I get back. Can we set a time?"

When I ran into them outside the chapel on 87th Street, they looked surprised. "We thought you didn't want to take the lessons?" one asked.

I smiled and said simply, "I changed my mind. Can I take them now?"

Their delighted "Yes!" felt like the opening of a new chapter in my life.

From that moment forward, opposition seemed to spring up everywhere. I learned quickly what I would later hear countless times: whenever you decide to follow the Lord, the adversary will be there too. "Satan seeketh that all men might be miserable like unto himself,' he and his followers try to lead us away from righteousness." But you and I have Agency, "Agency is a precious gift from God; it is essential to His plan for His children...Individuals do not have to give in to Satan's temptations. Each person has the power to choose good over evil, and the Lord has promised to help all who seek Him through sincere prayer and faithfulness." (Under Topics and Questions in the Gospel Library)

I had a choice: to turn to God in prayer and faithfulness, or to give in to doubt and fear.

I chose faith. And that choice rippled throughout every aspect of my life.

The first real hurdle came when the sister missionaries handed me over to the elders. The sisters had been my first point of contact in the Family Ward, and I felt comfortable with them. However, since I was a young single adult, they explained that it was best for me to take the lessons from the elders in the YSA ward. I didn't know these young men at all. Still, I wasn't about to let that stop me from progressing forward.

Three moments remain etched in my memory after I chose to take the lessons.

The first came when I was introduced to the Word of Wisdom. I'd always been a devoted coffee drinker, so when the elders explained that Latter-day Saints refrain from coffee and alcohol, my mind immediately rebelled. Alcohol wasn't a challenge, "It doesn't serve me anyhow," I said. But coffee? That was another story.

"How is coffee supposed to keep me away from the Savior?" I asked, half-defiant, half-genuinely curious.

I can't even recall their exact response. What I do remember is the undeniable impression I felt: follow the Word of Wisdom as you're preparing for baptism. That impression was stronger than any explanation. So, I quit coffee cold turkey.

When reading Jacob 7:3, I realized that you can "labor diligently" in the wrong work. I knew that I needed the Lord's help to know the difference between what would lead my heart astray and what would bring me closer to Him. That's why I chose to live the Word of Wisdom before I fully understood it. I trusted that obedience would bring understanding, and it did.

It wasn't easy. I quickly realized how much of a hold it had on me. Every time I walked past a coffee shop or instinctively reached to brew a cup, I had to stop and exercise choice. More than once, I prayed desperately for self-restraint. "Man," I thought, "I'm addicted to coffee. Who knew?"

In that struggle, the Lord opened my eyes. I began to see how often I had placed my faith in coffee instead of in Him. Whenever I needed energy or courage, I'd turn to caffeine instead of prayer. My old mantra had been, Give me a cup of coffee and I can do anything. But the Spirit gently showed me how many moments of divine help I had missed because I had chosen coffee over calling on Him.

As I kept the Word of Wisdom, the burden grew lighter. My love for the Lord deepened, and I felt His love for me in return. I realized it was never about the coffee itself. Nothing, no drink, no habit, could keep me from the Savior. It was about choosing to let His will prevail over mine. Each small sacrifice opened the way for His power to be present in my life.

Doctrine & Covenants 89 brought me peace: "And all saints who remember to keep and do these sayings, walking in obedience to the commandments, shall receive health in their navel and marrow to their bones; and shall find wisdom and great treasures of knowledge, even hidden treasures... And I, the Lord, give unto them a promise, that the destroying angel shall pass by them..."

It wasn't about what I was giving up. It was about what I was gaining.

I made a choice to act in accordance with His teachings, and He extended His power to me. Power to refrain from temptation.

But simply knowing isn't enough. We can study everything about seatbelts, but unless we actually put it on, it does us no good. On the other hand, someone may know very little about how it works, yet by applying it, they still receive the protection. The Temple works the same way. We may not fully understand how Temple worship shapes us to become more like God, but if we are willing to live the doctrine and apply it in our lives, the blessings will come. And as we keep asking, seeking, and knocking, the Lord will patiently teach us, line upon line, truth upon truth.

The second moment came when the missionaries told me, almost casually, that there was a living Prophet on the earth.

"Wait, what?" I blurted out.

"Yes," they said.

"You're telling me there are living Apostles and a living Prophet today, just like in the Bible?"

"Yes," they repeated.

I stared at them, stunned. "Then why isn't the Prophet on the front page of the New York Times?"

I couldn't comprehend that God had once again called a Prophet to guide His children. The thought was almost too big for me to hold. And yet, as I listened and studied, the Spirit confirmed it: Prophets and Apostles walk the earth today, teaching truth and testifying of Jesus Christ, just as in ancient times.

The final moment happened on a quiet evening, right before I was ready to set a baptismal date. I had just left a lesson and was walking home to my small apartment on 84th and 1st Avenue. It was dark, and the streets were mostly empty. I stopped under a lone streetlamp, its yellow glow spilling onto the sidewalk. Something in me froze.

I began questioning myself in silence: You felt like there was something missing from aspects of the Lutheran denomination, right?

"Yes," I admitted.

And the Baptist faith, as well?

"Yes."

Not even the non-denominational church you attended most recently felt like where you needed to be?

Another heavy "No."

I sank onto the edge of a planter box, staring blankly into the night. Then came the hardest question: Do you believe what The Church of Jesus Christ of Latter-day Saints is teaching?

Before I could even form an answer, a wave of fear and emptiness crashed over me. It felt like staring into an abyss. A tear slipped down my cheek, then another, until my vision blurred. In that instant, I believed in nothing. No church. No faith. No hope.

The despair was suffocating. I could barely breathe as I dragged myself across the street, climbed the five flights of stairs, and slipped quietly into my room so as not to wake my roommate. I knelt carefully, desperate and trembling, and prayed.

I don't recall the words I said. But at some point, I found myself at my desk, scriptures open before me. And there, in my mind's eye, I saw the streetlamp I'd been standing under. It was as though I could see myself still stuck down there in the darkness.

And then, light. Not the glow of the lamp, but a light within my soul. A confirmation so powerful, so personal, that I cannot fully write it here. But I know this: Jesus Christ is the Son of God. He lived, He taught, He died, and He rose again so that every soul, past, present, and future, could rise with Him. And return to be with our Father in Heaven just as Christ is.

I didn't just believe that. I knew it, with every fiber of my being.

From that night on, something in me shifted. I still didn't have money, and I was sleeping on a pile of old coats instead of a bed. I still had family struggles, broken relationships, and no romantic prospects. But I walked through the city with joy. My head was no longer down. I met eyes, smiled at strangers, and even greeted them. I felt lighter, almost as if I were skipping.

What had changed? Boyd K. Packer once said, "The study of the Doctrines of the Gospel will improve behavior quicker than a study of behavior will improve behavior." That's exactly what I was experiencing. The Doctrines and Principles of Jesus Christ were transforming me from the inside out.

I began to understand what the Savior meant in Matthew 7:20: "By their fruits ye shall know them." It's how His true Disciples are recognized, not just by what they say, but by how they live. I love how President Russell M. Nelson described it, in a talk titled, "A Plea to My Sisters." Describing women who follow the Savior will be "distinct and different, in happy ways, from the women of the world." You'll know them by their actions, their mindset, their choices, and the way they treat themselves and others.

A month later, I set the date for my baptism. My mom flew into New York, and together we drove to Nebraska for my cousin's wedding before returning for the big day.

Verses 6 and 12 in Ether 12, confirmed my decision beyond all doubt: "Faith is things which are hoped for and not seen... ye receive no witness until after the trial of your faith... For if there be no faith among the children of men, God can do no miracle among them."

And so, during the October General Conference weekend, between the morning and afternoon sessions, I entered the waters of baptism.

I had found my armor. I had chosen to put it on.

Chapter Three

— ✦ —

In The World Not of The World

"Wherefore, Brethren (And Sisters), Seek Not to Counsel the Lord, but to Take Counsel from His Hand. For Behold, Ye Yourselves Know That He Counseleth in Wisdom, And in Justice, And in Great Mercy, Over All His Works." -
JACOB 4:10

There I was, sitting at my computer in New York City, scanning flights to Utah and mapping out everything I'd need to make training for a Winter Olympic sport in Park City happen that November and December. That list was long, and it was on both sides of a white piece of printer paper. I felt so overwhelmed. Then I looked up at a sticky note that I had written and tapped to the side of my window, right in front of my desk. It read, "Seek to have spiritual experiences every day. Don't allow temporal concerns to displace spiritual priorities."

So, I took the advice to heart and began to pray. I thanked the Lord for the opportunity before me, and then simply asked: "If it's Thy will for me to spend a few months in Utah, please guide my steps and open the way, one moment at a time." Then, I went about my day.

In my early twenties, I learned that if you want to achieve something, you have to speak it out loud. Talking about your goals makes them real and invites others to help you bridge the gaps. So that's exactly what I did.

That evening was Institute, one of my favorite weekly gatherings, where a large group of young single adults came together to explore and discuss Gospel Principles. A survey of participants once revealed the top reasons young people attended: 1) to strengthen their relationship with Jesus Christ, 2) to grow spiritually, and 3) to gain confidence in making important life decisions. For me, it did all of that, and more.

That night, a bunch of my friends were there, and we all walked to the subway together to head home. As we talked, I began sharing my situation. I needed to find a way to move to Utah for two months. I'd never been there, and I didn't know a single person. But little by little, one miracle after another began to unfold. Just as I finished explaining my dilemma, my good friend responded without hesitation: "You could stay with my mom! She has a basement with a room and a kitchen; she'd love to have you. She lives in Provo, so you'd just need a car to get to and from Park City."

Then another friend jumped in: "I left my car in Provo! I could ask my parents to help get it set up for you to use while you're there."

My heart started to race. One by one, my friends began offering real solutions, including the names of people I could connect with out West, places to stay, and ways to make it all work. It was undeniable. I could feel the Lord's hand in it all, orchestrating answers I hadn't even thought to pray for.

That night, I went home and began checking boxes off my list. So many obstacles were cleared by my friends' suggestions, but a few significant ones remained. What would I say to my job? I couldn't afford to quit, and I couldn't afford to pay rent in both New York and Utah.

So I went back to my knees. I reminded myself not to worry, to trust. I gave it to the Lord- again. If it was meant to work out, I'd do all I could, and He would take care of the rest.

A week later, I finally gathered the courage to share my news with my investor and co-founder. We were seated around the long conference table in Greenwich, CT. The windows were open, letting in a soft breeze, and the sunlight streamed across the room. My investor and a few members of his family office sat across from me, while my co-founder was at my left.

Birds were chirping outside, so loudly that it was almost comical. I remember silently pleading with them to quiet down: Please, not now. I have big news to share.

The meeting wound down, chairs scraping as people prepared to leave, and panic surged in my chest. I stood quickly.

"One more thing before you all go," I blurted out, tilting my chin slightly downward to mask the nerves rattling inside me.

I took a steadying breath and delivered it as casually as I could, though I knew it would change everything:

"I'd like to move to Utah for two months and work remotely from there, still on East Coast hours, so I can train for the Skeleton in Park City. Would you all support me in doing that?"

I realized then my knees were locked, trembling so badly I thought I might collapse. My investor looked at me, eyebrows raised.

"Are you kidding me? You want us to support you while you try to make an Olympic team?"

My stomach flipped violently, and I was sure I might be sick. Then he broke into a grin.

"Yeah, you go for it!"

The room shifted. One by one, my team chimed in with encouragement, pats on the back, and wide smiles. Someone joked, "We'd better get to wear that medal when you win."

They were definitely putting the cart before the horse. I hadn't even tried the sport yet, but it didn't matter. I felt like Jello. Joyful, Jello.

I returned to my desk, whispered a prayer of thanks in my heart, and sat there in disbelief. The miracle wasn't just that they said yes, it was that they believed in me, maybe even before I fully believed in myself.

My co-founder had recently moved to Greenwich, CT, closer to our VC's office, while I commuted almost daily from the Upper East Side. One afternoon, he walked over to my desk and asked casually, "What are you doing with your apartment for those two months?"

I looked up, eyes widening. Could this really be another answer to prayer?

"Well, actually," I said slowly, "I'm looking for someone to rent it while I'm gone. Are you interested?"

"Yes," he replied. "Let's talk over lunch."

Once again, the Lord provided.

About three weeks later, I landed in Utah, suitcases in hand, equal parts excitement and nerves flooding through me. That first day blurred by, because that evening I was scheduled for my very first sliding practice at the Olympic Training Center in Park City.

Driving up the mountain, I was awestruck. I had never seen such majestic peaks, never stood on top of such vast beauty. I kept pulling over to snap pictures, whispering over and over, How great is our God. I felt so small in the best possible way.

When I arrived at the track, I checked in, suited up, and prepared to launch myself headfirst down a sheet of ice with my chin hovering an inch or two above the surface.

There is no true way to prepare for a life-shaking jolt like this. All I can say is: you can do hard things. And trying new things, good, worthwhile things, is always worth it.

I'd signed a waiver that essentially said if I died, it was on me. Questionable, yes. But standing at the start line, terrified yet resolute, I knew deep down: I can do this.

My first coach had a phrase he repeated endlessly, so often it felt burned into my brain:

"Embrace the hit."

At first, I thought it was just practical advice. When I found myself careening toward the wall, whether from a mistake or bad luck, he told me to relax and take it. Don't resist. Don't deflect. Accept the impact and let it push you forward.

So I tried. Over and over. I embraced the hit until my chin was split open, my pinky toe broken, and my arms bruised black and blue. I looked like I'd fought a gorilla. The pain was up close and personal.

More than once, I thought, Why not just brake? But there are no brakes in Skeleton. That option was never on the table.

One day, exasperated, I asked my coach, "What exactly am I supposed to notice?"

He said, "Watch how, when you embrace the hit, it spits you out onto a better path. It won't hold you against the wall as long. It even sets you up for the next turn, sometimes better than you could attempt."

My mind lit up. This wasn't just about Skeleton; it was about life.

That night, sore but burning with conviction, I went home to journal and pray. In the quiet, Heavenly Father added one more piece:

Embrace the hit, with Jesus Christ.

With Him, the pressure doesn't pin you against the wall as long. With Him, the pain is lightened. With Him, the hit can set you up for the next turn in ways you might never have prayed for or even imagined.

It's not natural to see pain rushing toward you and relax into it. Instinct tells you to steer away, to brace, to resist at all costs. And I'll be honest, I didn't always listen. I tried deflecting. But every time, it only made the pain worse, driving me harder into the wall and holding me there longer than I would like.

Slowly, I learned. Accepting the inevitable hit shortened the suffering and often realigned me onto a better course. Sometimes, surrendering to it was the only way to find the fastest, smoothest path forward, through it.

I began applying this lesson during my runs, and the results came. My times improved. My confidence grew. I was getting the hang of it, though I knew there was still so much left to learn.

Jeffrey R. Holland said, "In our present day, tremendously difficult issues face any Disciple of Jesus Christ.

We might sometimes want to run away from where we are, but we certainly should never run away from who we are, children of the living God who loves us, who is always ready to forgive us, and who will never, ever forsake us.

You are His most precious possession. You are His child, to whom He has given Prophets and promises, spiritual gifts and revelations, miracles and messages, and Angels on both sides of the veil.

In a world that so desperately needs all the light it can get, please do not minimize the eternal light God put in your soul before this world was."

One of the most profound and essential truths I know that strengthens me to embrace the hits in life with Jesus Christ is this: I am, and have always been, a daughter of God.

Many of us have heard the phrase, "I am a child of God." Perhaps you've even told someone else, "You are a son or daughter of the Most High God." But what fills my soul with the deepest joy is the extension of that truth: we have always been children of God. From the very beginning, before this life, and for all eternity, that has never changed.

Your choices can't change this, nor what you believe. It is who you are.

What I know with eternal certainty is that I have a Heavenly Father. A Father who had created an entire plan around me. And not just me, around you, too.

One of my favorite teachings on this subject comes from Elder Alan T. Phillips of the Seventy, as presented in the October 2023 General Conference. He began by quoting President Russell M. Ballard:

"There is one important identity we all share now and forever... That is that you are, and have always been, a son or daughter of God. Understanding this truth, really understanding it and embracing it, is life-changing."

Elder Phillips then added:

"Do not misunderstand or devalue how important you are to your Father in Heaven. You are not an accidental by-product of nature, a cosmic orphan, or the result of matter plus time plus chance. Where there is a design, there is a Designer. Your life has meaning and purpose. The ongoing Restoration of the Gospel of Jesus Christ brings light and understanding regarding your divine identity. You are a beloved child of Heavenly Father. You are the subject matter of all those parables and teachings. God loves you so much that He sent His Son to heal, rescue, and redeem you. Jesus Christ recognized the divine nature and eternal worth of each person."

That truth changes everything. It anchors us. It reminds us that no matter where we've been, what we've done, or how far we feel from God, we have never stopped being His children. And we never will.

I've come to learn that the act of embracing, truly opening your arms and heart to life, is rooted in hope. Not a shallow hope, but a hope born through progression, through the willingness to keep moving forward even when the path feels steep.

Heavenly Father has been teaching me, through the quiet whisperings of the Holy Ghost, why trials are not only inevitable but essential. They are not punishments; they are tutors. They refine us in ways comfort never could.

And in my darkest hours, I've found strength in remembering that Jesus Christ has already walked this road. He has felt every ache, every heart-shattering loss, every moment of despair I will ever know. He bore it all in His Atoning sacrifice, not in the abstract, but for me, for you, for every soul who would ever cry out in loneliness or pain.

It's here that I've come to understand the beauty of mercy and grace. Mercy is not getting what we deserve; grace is receiving what we never could deserve. Together, they weave a safety net strong enough to catch every one of us, no matter how far we fall.

Hope, I've realized, can ache. It stretches the soul; it exposes the places we feel most fragile. But faith, faith in Him, heals.

In Ether 12:27, the Lord declares, "If men come unto me I will show unto them their weakness. I give unto men weakness that they may be humble; and my grace is sufficient for all men that humble themselves before me... then will I make weak things become strong unto them." Weakness, in the Lord's eyes, is not condemnation; it is an invitation. Pride can appear as superiority, but it can also manifest as inadequacy when we see ourselves as less than others. In both cases, the Lord gently reminds us that wherever we are lacking, He can and will make up the difference if we will simply bring it to Him in humility.

So there I was, laying down every dream, every ambition, every hope of success in this new chapter of life. I placed them all at the Savior's feet and prayed with trembling humility: "Take this. Shape it. Make of it what You will. For I know You bring order to chaos and purpose to wandering." The truth is, none of us can move mountains on our own. It may only take a mustard seed of faith, but it takes His power to lift, to remove, or to help us climb the obstacles in our path.

And when the mountain doesn't move, when the waves keep rising higher despite our prayers, we must remember: it is not enough to simply look toward Him. We must reach for Him. We must clasp His hand with our effort and faith, while He lifts us with His power and grace.

Every valley forces us to look upward. Every burden stretches our capacity to receive more. Weakness turns to strength, sorrow to joy, if we allow Him to be part of the transformation.

As Doctrine & Covenants 88:32 teaches, "...enjoy that which they are willing to receive." He longs to give us more, more light, more truth, more strength, yet so often, I realize the gifts are already within my reach. The Temple stands near, His scriptures rest unopened on my nightstand, His presence hovers closer than I sometimes choose to notice. He is always ready to give.

The question is: where am I spending my time, and am I truly willing and prepared to receive?

Chapter Four

$$—\blacklozenge—$$

When Things Happen to You Struggles Pave the Way.
Progression with A Side of Trials

"Be One Who Nurtures and Who Builds. Be One Who Has an Understanding and A Forgiving Heart, Who Looks for The Best in People. Leave People Better Than You Found Them. Be Fair with Your Competitors, Whether in Business, Athletics, Or Elsewhere. Don't Get Drawn into Some of the Parlance of Our Day and Try to "Win" By Intimidation or by Undermining Someone's Character. Lend A Hand to Those Who Are Frightened, Lonely, Or Burdened." - Marvin J. Ashton

I want to begin by clearing something up. Have you ever found yourself saying, "Why did this have to happen to me?" Or maybe, "Of course this would happen to me," as if trouble had your name written all over it? Here's the truth: whatever that thing is you're going through, you're not alone. It's not just you, it's everyone. Every human who has lived, who lives now, and who will live. It's called life. In scripture, it's sometimes called a "probationary state."

Now, before we go any further, you might have stumbled a bit when I said fortunately instead of unfortunately. I chose that word deliberately. Because trials, though painful, can be a gift, they are not designed to break us, but to grow us. So I invite you, even now, to pause. Take a breath. Say a prayer to Heavenly Father in the name of Jesus Christ. Ask Him to help you understand why we need tribulations, and how they fit into His plan for our eternal salvation. This counsel does not apply to abuse. Abuse is never acceptable, under any circumstances. If you have experienced abuse, your Bishop and trusted counselors are there to help you take the necessary steps to ensure protection, healing, and prevention with the power of Jesus Christ.

If prayer feels foreign to you, let me offer a simple pattern. This is how I begin: I kneel, fold my arms, and say, "Dear Heavenly Father..." Then, in my own words, I speak reverently to Him, just as a child would to a loving parent. And when I'm ready to close, I end with, "In the name of Jesus Christ, Amen."

With the Holy Ghost as our guide, let's press forward and examine how these experiences, hard as they may be, are intended to help us. The Book of Mormon, in Alma, teaches that "mortality is a probationary state, a time of imperfect knowledge, when we learn by degrees, and show our commitment through righteous living. Alma teaches that only by keeping the commandments can we free ourselves from sin and enter the rest of the Lord."

None of this is possible without Jesus Christ. Believing in Him is part of the plan, but we also must act. We are here to progress. And to progress, we need these things: trials, opposition, resistance, the storms that test our roots.

For me, the first storm hit in fifth grade.

I was adopted when I was two months old, fresh from the hospital, placed in the arms of two people who chose me. My parents couldn't have children of their own, and I was their first living child. They loved me as if I had always been theirs, and in every way that mattered, I was.

Life felt steady. We moved to Texas when I was in second grade, built a beautiful home, and I thrived at a private Lutheran school while training as a competitive gymnast. My childhood felt idyllic: church on Sundays, a best friend just down the block, laughter echoing through our house.

And then, one day, I ran into my parents' bedroom while my mom was in the shower. My dad had already left for work. On the bed lay a book, its title in bold capital letters: DIVORCE.

But I didn't know that word. I read it as DIVISION. And my young mind leapt to the only conclusion it could: this must be about me. Math had never been my strongest subject. Maybe my parents thought I wasn't doing well enough in class. Shame burned in me as I stared at that word, believing I had let them down.

Not long after, they sat me down on the couch. With quiet voices and somber eyes, they told me they were getting a divorce. My world tilted. I had never seen them fight. Not once. No shouting matches, no slamming doors, no evidence of cracks in their marriage. To me, it came out of nowhere, like being struck in the face with a baseball I hadn't even seen coming.

As a child, you see the world only through your lens. It's not selfishness, it's just the only perspective you have. And from where I sat, everything revolved around me. So, naturally, I thought, "This is my fault." What did I do wrong? How can I fix this? If I promise to do better, will it go away?

Let me pause here and tell you what I wish someone had told me then: if you're a child caught in the middle of a divorce, it is not your fault. This is your parents' decision, not a reflection of your worth.

But I didn't know that yet. And in a blink, the three musketeers, my mom, dad, and I, were split apart. I went from feeling like we were a team to feeling like a ping pong ball, bouncing between two places but never truly at home in either.

My parents did their best. They loved me fiercely and tried to steady me. They showed up at gymnastics meets, asked about school, encouraged my curiosity, and my stubborn streak. They parented me the best way they knew how. Still, the fracture in our family left a mark.

And for years, I wrestled with loneliness, abandonment, and the aching question: Why me?

It took me decades to learn to forgive, not just my parents, but myself as well. Decades before, I stopped running from the pain, numbing it, or pretending it didn't exist. What finally changed me was turning to Jesus Christ. When I invited Him into my brokenness, the Holy Ghost began to gently guide me, showing me that man was never meant to be alone. That's why Heavenly Father sent His Son, not just to redeem us, but to be with us.

Through prayer, through scripture, through countless tearful nights, I learned that I didn't have to carry it all. On my knees, I confessed my anger, my fear, my desperate attempts to control what was never mine to fix. And in return, He gave me something I didn't deserve:

peace. That is mercy, not getting what we do deserve. And grace, that's receiving blessings we never could deserve.

Slowly, He showed me how to re-focus. How to see that even in trials, I was not forgotten. Even when I felt abandoned, He was right there. I realized I had been echoing Laman and Lemuel's words in 1 Nephi 3:5: "It is a hard thing which [has been] required of [me]."

Yes, it was hard. But in Christ, I found that hard things were not meant to destroy me. They were meant to refine me.

Trials come to every one of us, but how we meet them determines what they leave behind. Every hardship presents a choice: will I let this soften me, or will I let it harden me? Trials demand a response. You can grow, or you can shrink. But before you choose, let me remind you of who you truly are.

You, yes, you, are a child of the Most High God. The King of all that was, is, and will ever be. You are the brother or sister of His Only Begotten Son, the pure and perfect Messiah, the Prince of Peace, the Savior of the world, Jesus Christ. As Heavenly Father's heir, you carry within you divine potential if you will rise up and become what He designed you to be. He has perfect faith in you. He knows you completely. He loves you without measure. If you let the Holy Ghost be your constant companion, you can grow into your celestial self through Christ.

I'll never forget something my first senior missionary couple told me in New York City, in the YSA ward. They had a way of bringing eternal truths down to earth. One evening in Institute class, she pointed out a phrase that is repeated throughout the scriptures: "It came to pass." Not that it came to stay. The word of God is filled with stories of famine, war, captivity, loss, family strife, and struggles of faith. But none of those things were permanent. They did not come to stay; they came to pass. So when you are walking through darkness, remember: it's a season, not your eternity.

I once came across a line in Napoleon Hill's Think and Grow Rich that struck me with piercing clarity: "Every adversity brings with it the seed of an equivalent advantage." The scriptures testify to the same truth. When we make God our partner and trust the Great Gardener, He takes the shears in hand. He prunes, cuts, and trims away what cannot stay. He buries what must die so that something greater may live. And then, He waters, He nourishes, He tends with infinite care. In His hands, even our seasons of loss become soil for abundance.

That is how you go from powerless to Power-in-us. Because God the Father, Jesus Christ, and the Holy Ghost are already the perfect team. They know your strengths and weaknesses better than you do. They already know how to work with you. All they ask is that you meet with them daily:

Review your life with them.

Repent in the name of Jesus Christ.

Re-Focus with the help of the Holy Ghost.

That pattern, Review, Repent, Re-Focus, is how I turn to Him when I feel like I have lost my way. "Remission of sins is made possible by the Atonement of Jesus Christ. A person obtains a remission of his sins if he (she) has faith in Christ, repents of his (her) sins, receives the ordinances of baptism and laying on of hands for the gift of the Holy Ghost, and obeys God's commandments." (Under Guide to the Scriptures on churchofjesuschrist.org).

And remission isn't just about forgiveness. I once heard it described like this: Remission = Remember your mission. Because when you Review, Repent, and Re-Focus, you realize that your sins are not only forgiven, they are forgotten by the Lord. He does not hold them against you. He doesn't throw them back in your face. He erases them, so you can move forward clean and free. Daniel Rona said, "Repentance can turn sin into experience."

And let's not forget, you chose this path. Before you came to earth, you chose to follow Jesus Christ. Every person with a body made that choice when we lived with our Divine family in the pre-existence. We knew it would be hard. We knew it would test us. But we also knew it would refine us into beings more like our Savior. And we knew the most important truth of all: the battle for our souls had already been won. Jesus Christ had already chosen to suffer, to die, and to rise again, so that we too could be resurrected, body and spirit reunited in glory.

So don't pray yourself off the path too quickly. The learning is in the obstacles. And they were never meant to be tackled alone.

I learned that firsthand in my early twenties. I had just graduated from Baylor University and spent a year saving everything I could before finally making the leap to New York City. At the time, I was living in a tumultuous situation with family, constant fighting, sharp words, and very little love to be found. I had prayed countless times for a way out, for a chance to start fresh in New York. But on paper, it was impossible. I had no money. No support waiting for me in the city. Just a burning desire to go, and the determination to do hard things well.

Then one day in 2012, while scrolling Vogue.com, I stumbled across a sweepstakes. It was called "Vogue American Beauty." The prompt was simple: submit an essay on "What American Beauty Means to Me."

I didn't think much of it. I wasn't expecting anything. But the words came easily:

"American beauty doesn't just derive from where you come from. Its authenticity originates from each woman's accomplishments, setbacks, and her rare, effortless outlook on herself and life. I am half African American, half Swedish. I am also adopted, and my adoptive mother is Thai, and my father is Black. Being bi-racial and adopted into a mixed family reflects a melting pot of modern American beauty. It embodies the acceptance of myself, loving the differences of others around me, and the confidence to proudly portray that I'm a representation of my soul, not my skin. I do not fit into a stereotype."

I submitted the essay, along with a photo, and promptly forgot about it. For me, it was more about the joy of writing, the thrill of playing with words that tasted true on my tongue. Still, the prize wasn't bad: two round-trip tickets to New York during Fashion Week, a stay at the Mark Hotel across from the Met, a private tour of Assouline Publishing, signed books from Claiborne Swanson Frank, a shopping spree at Neiman Marcus, front-row seats to a fashion show, and a chauffeured Mercedes to whisk me through the city.

At the time, it felt like a dream far too big to belong to me. But as I was learning then, and have seen countless times since, God specializes in making the impossible possible.

A few weeks slipped by, and my home was simmering toward a boiling point with no return. The air was thick with contention; moods were sharp, brittle, and ready to shatter. I did everything I could to escape the tension, waking earlier than everyone else, slipping quietly out the door, and heading to hot yoga before work. If someone was up at 5 a.m., I'd leave at 4:30 a.m. just to avoid the storm.

But one morning, I overslept. And that was the morning it all exploded. Words turned into daggers. Shouts filled the house. The fight ended with a sentence that carved itself into me like stone:

"Get your things and take them with you, you're not allowed back here."

Just like that, I was kicked out.

I drove to work with rage and grief warring inside me, my hands trembling on the steering wheel. In the parking lot, I sat in my car dialing homeless shelters. Every single one told me the same thing: doors locked at a certain hour, long before my shift ended. There was no place for me.

The floodgates burst open. I wept in the car, my chest heaving, and prayed, more desperately than I ever had in my life. It felt like I was drowning, choking under dark water, begging the Lord to lift me up before I sank completely.

Then, my phone rang. It was my best friend in Los Angeles. The moment she heard my voice, she knew. I told her, through sobs, what had happened. She paused and said, "Hold on, I'll call you right back." Minutes later, another text lit up my screen:

"You're staying with me. Come as soon as you're off work."

I broke down again, this time with tears of relief. It was a miracle. Heavenly Father was reminding me that He often blesses His children through the hands of others.

But the day wasn't finished with me yet. Later, during my shift, I checked my phone. Two missed calls from a New York number. And then, an email:

"Congratulations, you have won the Vogue American Beauty Sweepstakes!"

I couldn't believe it. Hours earlier, I had been on the floor of despair, certain I had lost everything. Now, I was staring at a door to a dream I'd barely dared hope for. Right there in the break room, in front of coworkers who must have wondered what on earth was happening, I dropped to my knees. I sobbed, not with sorrow this time, but with a humility and gratitude so full it burned through me. How grateful I was that He extended this tender mercy to me.

That day remains a monument in my life. A reminder that miracles are real. They may not come when or how we expect, but they come, always according to God's will. As Doctrine & Covenants 63:9–10 teaches:

"Faith cometh not by signs, but signs follow those that believe... signs come by faith, not by the will of men, nor as they please, but by the will of God."

And Moroni's words ring even truer for me now:

"Ye receive no witness until after the trial of your faith." (Ether 12:6)

Looking back, I see it so clearly: every choice I made, every heartbreak I endured, every door slammed in my face, all of it was preparing me. The Lord was shaping me, pruning me, positioning me exactly where I needed to be, with the heart I needed to have.

As Paul declared in Romans 8:28:

"And we know that all things work together for good to them that love God, to them who are called according to His purpose."

That day, my lowest valley became the soil for one of my greatest miracles.

It wasn't until my thirties that the Lord gently pulled back a corner of the veil and revealed an eternal truth.

As I've mentioned, my story includes a patchwork of parents, birth parents who gave me life, adoptive parents who raised me, and eventually stepparents who entered the picture after my adoptive parents remarried. With all those branches, you'd think I might feel rootless. But shortly after my baptism, I became captivated, no, consumed, by family history. Every Wednesday, without fail, I'd head to the Family History Center on the Upper West Side, sometimes spending over three hours building my tree, adding names, and chasing down stories.

I didn't expect it to feel the way it did. There was a joy, a plenitude of it, that flowed through me every time I found someone. A senior missionary couple serving in New York City as Family History missionaries taught me something that would become my spiritual compass for this work: "Pray before you begin. Ask to find those ready to make and keep covenants with the Lord and receive ordinances."

So I did, every time. And every time, I found someone. Whether from my birth line, my adoptive family, or even through my stepparents, there was always someone waiting.

The miracles from that season could fill a book, but there are two that I feel impressed to share.

The first came after I got married and finally discovered who my birth parents were. As I traced my birth mother's lineage, I learned that she was a descendant of the Prophet of the Restoration, Joseph Smith himself. Her side of the family was full of pioneers, men and women who helped build the early Church in Salt Lake City. That bloodline had been quietly beating in me all along, and the Spirit bore witness to the divine legacy that had waited patiently for me to uncover it.

Years later, while attending an endowment session in the Manti Temple, I was given a sacred vision. My husband and I were seated quietly, with only a handful of others in attendance. As I glanced toward the section of empty chairs to the left, I suddenly saw them filled—rows upon rows of people sitting in peace, clothed in joy, their countenances radiant with love. The image was so clear, so distinct, that I recorded it in my journal before letting time and life move me forward.

It was not until several years later that the meaning of that vision became clear. In my family history research, I discovered the first of my ancestors who had faithfully followed the Prophet's counsel and journeyed to America. Their path eventually led them to Manti, where they were sealed for time and all eternity in that very temple, the first sealing of my family line in the restored Church of Jesus Christ.

In that moment of discovery, the vision returned to me. I knew without doubt that the people I had seen were my ancestors, those who had made sacred covenants with the Lord and whose faith and sacrifice had blessed generations, including my own. The sweetness of that realization penetrated my soul. How grateful I am for those who came before me, for their courage, devotion, and consecrated labor in building the Kingdom of God. Their faithfulness was not only for their own salvation, but for all who would come after them.

The second miracle was even more astonishing. I learned that I had a half-sister, just eleven months older than me, who had also been placed for adoption by her birth mother. Unbelievably, we were both sent to the same adoption agency. But no one ever told the social workers that we were related, and we were adopted into separate families, growing up completely unaware of each other's existence.

That changed when she applied to be part of a television show about reuniting lost family members. The producers found me. We met for the first time on camera. That moment, our reunion, is now a television episode. She is incredible. Through her, we discovered that we share seven other half-siblings.

When I look back at the ripple effects of my parents' divorce, I see more than pain; I see the light that the Lord gave me to walk through it. Through family history work, I've helped locate six generations. I've learned their names, their stories. I've come to understand my place in the tapestry of it all. What an indescribable gift that has been.

To this day, I remain the only member of the Church in my family, outside of the family my husband and I are raising together. And sometimes I wonder if, in the pre-existence, I stood beside my Heavenly Father, Jesus Christ stood on His right, and the Father looked at me with love and said, "Courtney, I have important work for you. It won't be easy. But if you choose it, you're exactly the one I need."

And maybe, just maybe, I looked into my Father's eyes, then turned to Jesus and asked, "He's going first, right?"

The Lord nodded. Yes.

And with a steady smile, I answered, "Then yes. I'll follow Him."

Accepting the weight of my parents' decision, the breaking apart of what I thought was whole, took years. First came the resistance. Then came the surrender. And in that sacred, quiet surrender, Jesus Christ began to tutor me through the Spirit. This healing wasn't born of mere hope. It came through the hard, daily work of choosing a new perspective.

And through it all, I learned that even broken stories carry divine assignments.

Embracing this hit with Jesus Christ illuminated my testimony of just how profound family history work truly is, it is the greatest work on earth.

Chapter Five

─── ✦ ───

Live as for Years

"If Ye Are Prepared, Ye Shall Not Fear." - Doctrine & Covenants 38:30

To "live as for years" means to live with intention, even when life feels uncertain. It's about choosing to plant roots, showing up with faith, and building a life, not just waiting for one to happen. It's acting with the kind of trust in the Lord that says, "Even if this is temporary, I will treat it as sacred. I will give it my all."

For me, that's exactly what embracing the hit has looked like. Whether the hit was unexpected, difficult, or divine, I learned that I couldn't just sit in survival mode and wait for the next chapter. I had to choose faith now. I had to live as if the Lord's promises were already unfolding, even when I couldn't see them yet.

That meant settling into the present with purpose. Loving people. Making Covenants. Doing the work. Letting roots go down into whatever soil I was given and trusting that God would cause it to grow.

Living as for years is a spiritual posture, one of faith, commitment, and hope. And it's how I learned to embrace each hit not as a hindrance, but as part of my divine preparation.

By this point, I had been training and competing in Skeleton for nearly two years, splitting my time between the icy tracks of Park City during winter and the pulse of New York City during the off-season. It was Autumn in the city, my favorite time of year, and as I packed to head back west, I decided, somewhat impulsively, to download a dating app.

As a young Latter-day Saint woman, I was ready. I'd dated many men in New York, but nothing had truly clicked. I hoped, maybe this time, I'd find someone who would change everything for the better.

The night before the 2016 Presidential Election, I matched with someone. We made plans to meet the next day, just after I voted, at a café on the Upper East Side. I arrived a little early, expectant, nervous. Then I saw him walk through the door with luggage.

My eyes widened. My heart sank.

Oh no. He's homeless. This isn't a date. He's going to ask me for a place to stay.

I nearly stood up and walked out before he could spot me. But he did. And with a confident smile, he walked over and sat down.

"Hi," I said, still trying to make sense of the situation. "What's with the luggage?"

He laughed. "I fly out today."

Relief.

"Oh! Where to?" I asked, heart rate finally stabilizing.

"Mississippi. That's where I live."

Mississippi? My head tilted, processing. "Wait, you live in Mississippi? Then, why are you in New York?"

He explained that he'd come to the city with a friend for a concert and, for the first time ever, decided to download a dating app. We matched, so he squeezed in this last-minute date before heading to the airport.

I decided to stay, figuring we'd never see each other again. I'd never been to Mississippi, and my work took me mostly to Los Angeles. But he was kind and charming. We shared stories and dreams, laughed through brunch, and the date flew by.

When it ended, I realized something odd: he never asked for my number.

Guess he wasn't interested, I thought. Was I that forgettable?

Still, I gave myself a goal: If he's still standing outside when I get to the corner, I'll go back and ask to stay in touch.

He was. I turned around.

"Do you want to be friends online?" I asked.

His head snapped up. "I meant to ask for your number! Can we exchange numbers?"

"Yes," I smiled. "I'd like that."

Before we parted ways, I told him I'd be moving to Utah for two or three months the following week.

He blinked in surprise. "No way, I'll be there too, helping my parents move. Can we go out while you're there?"

"Definitely. I'll let you know once I'm in town." And we went on our separate ways.

As I prepared to leave for Utah, something stirred within me, something I couldn't ignore. I had spent over a year doing Temple work for my deceased ancestors, serving as proxy for Baptisms and Confirmations. But now I felt called to do more.

One thought pressed gently but clearly in my mind: Why not receive your Endowment so you can perform more ordinances on behalf of them?

The joy that accompanied that impression was undeniable.

I began thinking about the steps I'd need to take. I would talk to my Bishop, take the Temple Preparation class, and prepare myself.

"The word endow has two related meanings: 'to bestow a gift' and 'to clothe upon.' In this context, the Temple Endowment is a sacred gift whereby we are clothed with blessings from God now and forever."

The blessings promised through the Endowment are immense: greater knowledge, divine power, guidance, protection, and lasting peace.

That verse from Doctrine and Covenants 51:16-17 popped into my mind, "as for years."

"I consecrate unto them this land for a little season, until I, the Lord, shall provide for them otherwise, and command them to go hence; And the hour and the day is not given unto them, wherefore let them act upon this land as for years, and this shall turn unto them for their good."

"To live as for years", to me, it felt like the Lord's version of carpe diem, but with an Eternal lens. It's a divine invitation to seize the day not in haste or impulse, but with purpose, with faith, and with a forward-facing heart. We weren't sent here to merely pass the time. As hymn 226 beautifully puts it, we are meant to "improve the shining moments," to recognize that eternity is made up of the choices we make in each of these small, sacred hours.

But just as quickly as I embraced this hit of inspiration, a dark cloud settled over me.

Suddenly, an overshadowing was cast over my sunny enthusiasm: "You're not worthy."

"You haven't been a member long enough. You're not ready."

The joy drained from my spirit. Doubt crept in, and I began closing my family tree tabs on the computer. Who did I think I was to do this work?

Weeks passed. I didn't have my usual delight in attending Institute, I found myself avoiding family history work, and barely listening at church.

Then, one Sunday in Relief Society, we were studying the life of President Howard W. Hunter in "Teachings of Presidents of the Church," and one sentence jolted me awake:

"Let's not take counsel from our fears."

That line pierced the fog. I went home that afternoon and dove into my scriptures. I read 1 Nephi 3:7:

"...I will go and do the things which the Lord hath commanded, for I know that the Lord giveth no commandments unto the children of men, save he shall prepare a way for them that they may accomplish the thing which he commandeth them."

Tears filled my eyes as the truth settled deep in my heart: I am worthy to do this work, because of Jesus Christ. His grace had made a way for me, and I knew I didn't have to navigate it alone. My Bishop would help me understand what came next.

Without hesitation, I picked up my phone and sent a message to the Bishop's secretary:

"Can I schedule a meeting with the Bishop?"

I didn't want to wait another day. I was ready to act on this good desire the Lord had placed in my heart.

I think of it this way: when we waste time, it only delays blessings. This life matters. This season matters. Even if it feels like a temporary stop along the way, the Lord asks us to act upon this land as for years, to treat the now as holy, to show up fully, to plant, to build, to love, to grow.

And I don't believe that counsel was meant only for early Saints setting down roots in new places. I believe it was given for all of us, anyone navigating uncertainty, waiting on promises, or wondering if this exact moment matters.

Because it does.

On December 17, 2016, I received my Endowment in the House of the Lord. It remains one of the most sacred days of my life.

With the memory of my Endowment fresh in my heart and my move to Utah underway, I made a goal: to visit as many temples as I could while I was there.

And the person who volunteered to make that happen, driving me, scheduling everything?

The same man I met that day on the Upper East Side.

President Gordon B. Hinckley once said, "Marriage will be the most important decision of your life... Marry the right person in the right place at the right time."

And Elder Bruce R. McConkie taught that we should seek a companion "who is living so that he or she can go to the Temple of God and make the Covenants that we there make."

About a year and a half later, that remarkable man and I were sealed in the San Antonio Temple.

When I find myself wrestling with spiritual decisions, confused about what's Doctrine and what's Principle, I remember this:

Doctrine is the "why."

Principles are the "what."

If we focus only on the how, without understanding the why or the what, we risk missing the mark entirely.

I knew how to perform the work for my ancestors, but when I prayed to understand why we do that work and what it meant for them, my heart softened, and I began to see His will.

Not every 'hit' in life is a setback or a detour into disappointment. Some hits are Heavenly, sacred gifts disguised as turning points, divine in nature and eternal in purpose. Both versions you might not see coming, but bear the opportunity to awaken us, redirect us, and gently push us forward on the Covenant path. Choosing to progress within the Lord's Plan of Happiness and following my Savior didn't just heal my past; it opened me up to a future rooted in faith. Faith in my Savior and Heavenly Father's Plan of Salvation.

By learning to follow spiritual promptings, by heeding the words of our living Prophet, and by making time to stand in holy places, especially the Temple, the house of the Lord, I began to see that preparing for blessings isn't a passive hope. It's an active, daily practice.

Just as I said before, from David A. Bednar, "Faith is the principle of action and then power. The sequence is first we act in accordance with the teachings of the Savior, then we are blessed with His power."

And one of the sweetest blessings that came from this sacred alignment was meeting my dear, eternal companion.

President Russell M. Nelson taught:

"Increase your understanding of priesthood power and of Temple Covenants and blessings. Having places of security to which you can retreat will help you embrace the future with faith."

He continued:

"Let us not just endure this current season. Let us embrace the future with faith! Turbulent times are opportunities for us to thrive spiritually. There are times when our influence can be much more penetrating than in calmer times."

Those words weren't just comforting, they were instructional. Strengthening spiritual safety nets by doing the small and simple things isn't only about protection; it's about preparation. And as I learned to repent daily, to clear space for the Spirit, and to trust in sacred Covenants, I came to believe his prophetic promise:

"I promise that as we create places of security, prepare our minds to be faithful to God, and never stop preparing, God will bless us. He will 'deliver us; yea, insomuch that he [will] speak peace to our souls, and [will] grant unto us great faith, and ... cause us that we [can] hope for our deliverance in him.'"

I have felt that peace. I have tasted that hope. And I know, with my whole soul, that the "hits" of life, when offered to Christ, become the very tools He uses to shape our future with faith.

Elder David A. Bednar reminds us that "such antagonism is not new.

In 1861, as the Salt Lake Temple was being built, Brigham Young encouraged the Saints: "If you wish this Temple built, go to work and do all you can. ... Some say, 'I do not like to do it, for we never began to build a Temple without the bells of hell beginning to ring.' I want to hear them ring again. All the tribes of hell will be on the move, ... but what do you think it will amount to? You have all the time seen what it has amounted to."

Bednar continues with, "We as faithful Saints have been strengthened by adversity and are the recipients of the Lord's tender mercies. We have moved forward under the promise of the Lord: "I will not suffer that [mine enemies] shall destroy my work; yea, I will show unto them that my wisdom is greater than the cunning of the devil," found in Doctrine & Covenants 10:43 □.

Bednar aligns this with, "the paralleled promises contained in the dedicatory prayer offered upon the Kirtland Temple in 1836: "We ask thee, Holy Father, to establish the people that shall worship, and honorably hold a name and standing in this thy house, to all generations and for eternity; That no weapon formed against them shall prosper; that he who diggeth a pit for them shall fall into the same himself. That no combination of wickedness shall have power to rise up and prevail over thy people upon whom thy name shall be put in this house; and if any people shall rise against this people, that thine anger be kindled against them. And if they shall smite this people thou wilt smite them; thou wilt fight for thy people as thou didst in the day of battle, that they may be delivered from the hands of all their enemies," found in Doctrine & Covenants 109:24-28.

Bednar leaves this talk with this: "Please consider these verses in light of the current raging of the adversary and what we have discussed about our willingness to take upon us the name of Jesus Christ and the blessing of protection promised to those who honorably hold a name and standing in the Holy Temple. Significantly, these covenant blessings are to all generations and for all Eternity. I invite you to study repeatedly and ponder prayerfully the implications of these scriptures in your life and for your family."

Chapter Six

— ✦ —

If You're Tired of Standing, Kneel

"You Are Called for Who You Are, Not for Who You Are Not"

"Pray He is there. "Pray to know. Pray to grow. Pray to show," President Susan H. Porter continued. President Russell M. Nelson has invited you to 'pour out your heart to your Heavenly Father... And then listen!' Listen to what you feel in your heart and to thoughts that come to your mind."

As newlyweds building our life in New York City, my husband moved into my apartment, and we were both working and praying toward the following steps: a new job for him, a new place to live, and the future we felt called to create together. We fasted often and took our questions to the Temple. One evening, we booked an Endowment session at the newly dedicated Hartford, Connecticut, Temple to close a fast we'd been doing for his job search.

As the session began, my mind should've been still. Focused. Reverent. But a thought kept intruding. And not just once, it kept buzzing back like a fruit fly, persistent and annoying:

Broadcast journalism.

Over and over again.

Broadcast journalism? I thought. Why? That makes no sense. I have a job I love. I'm co-building a company with my co-founder. We've secured venture capital. I'm committed for at least another year. Where is this coming from?

Yes, I had a degree in News/Editorial Journalism from Baylor, but I had given up working in broadcast. And yet the prompting wouldn't go away. It distracted me the entire session. I felt almost guilty that I couldn't focus on the sacred Ordinances taking place.

Later, in the Celestial Room, I turned to my husband and whispered, "I kept getting this strong impression to apply for broadcast journalism jobs."

He raised an eyebrow, surprised. "I'm the one fasting for job inspiration," he laughed.

We got home, and while he started dinner, I opened my laptop and called into the kitchen, "What do you think that was all about? Should I actually search for something?"

He called back, without missing a beat, "Maybe it means... You should look for broadcast journalism jobs!"

Point taken.

So I typed just that into the search engine: "Broadcast journalism jobs." One of the top results was for an on-air TV host with a home shopping network. I clicked on the listing, casually reading through the description. Line after line, I found myself saying, Yeah, I could do that. I've done something similar. I can learn that. Before I had time to second-guess myself, I submitted an application. I closed my laptop and we went on with our night.

Two weeks later, I got an email. The casting director wanted me to submit two short videos selling products I loved. Thankfully, I had plenty of wedding gifts to choose from. I filmed the videos using my phone, balanced precariously on a thermostat in our fitness-tech startup's empty studio. I featured two items: my electric kettle and a glass jewelry box. With time short and my schedule tight, I submitted both videos in a single take.

A few weeks later, I was invited to an in-person audition in lower Manhattan. And soon after that, I was stunned to learn I'd been selected, one of six chosen out of 17,000 applicants.

But the biggest twist? The job would require moving to West Chester, Pennsylvania.

My husband had only been living in New York City for four months. Yet, without hesitation, we packed up our things and headed to the land of our forefathers, and Amish donuts.

Looking back, I'm amazed by how clearly God's hand was guiding me. What I initially dismissed as a distraction in the Temple turned out to be a powerful prompting. As Elder Dale G. Renlund taught:

"Revelation requires similar concentration and elimination of distractions. To receive personal revelation, we need to walk away from worldly noise... Rather, we create an environment that fosters feeling and recognizing the Spirit."

I believe that because we had fasted, sought the Spirit, and chose to stand in Holy places, I was beginning to learn how the Spirit speaks to me, even if I didn't recognize it in the moment. I was prepared. And the prompting found its way in.

President Camille N. Johnson beautifully taught:

"God knows you. He knows your situation. He knows your heart. Trust in the Lord, learn to hear His voice, and then go forward with confidence and relief. He needs you in His work."

And He needed me in this new season of life.

My husband's willingness to support the prompting, not just humor it, but truly encourage me to act, was a blessing all its own. I once heard a professor in Provo say something that's stayed with me:

"When obedience ceases to be an irritant and becomes our quest, then we are near the Spirit. The opposite of obedience isn't disobedience, it's rebellion."

Our goal wasn't perfection, but progress. To obey with an open heart. To act in faith even when the path didn't make sense on paper. That's how the Lord trains us, through small promptings that teach big lessons.

As 2 Nephi 2:16 reminds us:

"Wherefore, the Lord gave unto man that he should act for himself."

And to act, we must have choices, real, opposing options. Faith is choosing the unfamiliar path simply because we feel Him beckoning us toward it.

That night in the Temple, I thought I was distracted.

But the Spirit was speaking.

And because we had prepared, I was able to embrace the hit, and follow Him.

About three years into my role as a TV host, and still training intensely for Skeleton, I could feel something shifting. I assumed it was the natural tension building before the National team trials and, not far behind, the Olympic Trials. I had an American flag pinned to the wall in our bedroom, right across from my bed, so it was the first thing I'd see each morning. It was more than decoration; it was a daily reminder of the goal I was chasing.

But chasing it was beginning to feel more complex than ever.

I worked overnight shifts on air, arriving at the studio at midnight and wrapping around 4:30 a.m. From there, I'd drive my husband to the train station so he could begin his grueling 2.5-hour commute into New York City. I'd sleep until about 1 p.m., then head to the gym for two hours, sometimes more. Some days, I'd come off a night shift only to jump straight into an afternoon shift later that same day, pushing my body to the point of staying up for over 36 hours at a time.

My husband and I became two ships passing in the night. Exhausted. Determined. Distant.

Then the world stopped.

The Global Pandemic hit, and suddenly, everything we knew as routine was suspended. We were locked down in our apartment, part confused, part fearful, and strangely, part hopeful. This was a hit no one could've predicted. It rippled through every corner of our lives. We prayed for sick loved ones, grieved with friends, fasted for peace during political unrest, and tried to make sense of what it meant to wait while the world hurt.

The Pandemic wasn't just opposition. For many, it was devastation. And yet, in my personal prayers, desperate and searching, I kept asking to see the Lord's hand in it all. To invite Him into this unimaginable, collective hit. What I found wasn't immediate peace, but a deep, Sacred stillness. A Holy quiet that reminded me that God, my Father, and Jesus Christ, my Savior, are my divine family. And they had not abandoned us.

My husband and I clung to the counsel of our Prophet, President Russell M. Nelson, who taught us how to transform our homes into sanctuaries, where Sacred time and Holy space could coexist. We began to study Come, Follow Me faithfully and transformed our apartment into a Temple of learning, worship, and connection.

Elder David A. Bednar articulated:

"I promise that as we build the foundation of our lives on the 'rock' of Jesus Christ, we can be blessed by the Holy Ghost to receive an individual and spiritual stillness of the soul that enables us to know and remember that God is our Heavenly Father, we are His children, Jesus Christ is our Savior, and we can be blessed to do and overcome hard things." That stillness carried us through the news that the Olympic Trials would be postponed.

And in that unexpected space of slowed momentum, I found out I was pregnant.

It was beautiful, humbling news, joyous and sacred. We had just moved to another state to be closer to family during the Pandemic. It felt like a fresh start and a divine surprise all in one. We planned to tell our families over

Christmas, to celebrate the life that was beginning, this sweet, growing promise.

But two days before Christmas, everything changed.

I began cramping. Then bleeding. And within a few hours, we learned that I was having a miscarriage.

There are hits in life that you see coming, and then there are the ones that level you. This was the latter. It was more than a wave; it was a drowning. I felt like I was paddling through an endless ocean with no shore in sight. And in that silent, sinking grief, I learned something I never expected:

Hope can hurt.

To hope for something good and not understand why it couldn't be yours, at least not right now, was its own kind of ache. I wrestled with the Lord in prayer, searching for meaning, for relief, for something I could hold on to. And then, weeks later, a quiet phrase began repeating in my mind:

"That all these things shall give thee experience."

It settled into my heart slowly, like rain softening dry ground.

Through this pain, I gained a deeper compassion for parents and for the unseen weight so many carry. My heart expanded in unexpected ways. Women I barely knew began to share their stories with me, stories of loss, of healing, of resilience, and miracles. It was as if Heaven opened a channel of connection through sorrow, and strangers became sisters in a sacred community of remembrance.

I loved these women before I ever knew their names. As they laid their offerings at the feet of the Savior, I could feel their gladness and heartbreak as if they were my own. In that sacred space of shared vulnerability, something inside me began to shift. I began to heal, too.

There is power in listening to others while you yourself are learning to listen and embrace the hit.

In that season, I came to understand a spiritual gift I had once overlooked. Doctrine & Covenants 46:14 says:

"To others it is given to believe on their words, that they also might have eternal life if they continue faithful."

Before this, I had always connected more with the verse just before it, verse 13:

"To some it is given by the Holy Ghost to know that Jesus Christ is the Son of God, and that He was crucified for the sins of the world."

That had always felt like me. I knew Jesus was the Christ. I knew He Atoned for me. But in this season, the ache was too close, too raw. I couldn't bring myself to say aloud what I had once declared so freely. The grief had muted my voice. But even then, I didn't lose my way. Instead, I leaned on the light of others. I let their testimonies guide me while mine lay quiet. I borrowed their light like oil in my lamp, just enough to get through one more step in the dark.

And while I wrestled through the heaviness, the Savior didn't rush me. He met me in the depths. He pulled me close, held me up, and lifted me gently back to the foundation I had laid long before, that solid bedrock of Testimony in Jesus the Christ. Then, like a loving Father, He let me rest there. He waited until I was ready to rise again and continue the lifelong work of gathering spiritual light.

To truly exercise our Agency, we must face opposition. We must stand in the tension between what is and what we hope will be. We must choose, again and again, between despair and devotion, between turning inward and turning to the Lord.

And though this particular season of sorrow brought anguish I had never imagined, it also brought with it a sacred offering: my first child, unborn.

In the quiet aftermath, I caught the faintest glimpse of what it might have felt like for Heavenly Father to offer His Only Begotten Son. The ache. The surrender. The holiness of sacrifice. And while my offering was different, it was no less Sacred. I gave a tiny spirit a body. However small or unfinished it may have been, it was a beginning. A Sacred gift. A divine collaboration between mother, father, and Heaven.

Now, that little one is on the other side of the veil, doing a great and noble work I cannot yet see. One day, I'll know. One day, I'll hold them again, and I believe with all my soul that the joy of that reunion will be beyond anything I can now comprehend.

For now, I move forward, not with all the answers, but with a quiet kind of faith. I've learned that trust in God is not loud. It's steady. It's the gentle resolve to keep walking when you're not sure where the road will lead. And it's the Sacred assurance that His timing is not just good, it's perfect.

I respect my Father's plan.

The word respect itself teaches me how. When you break it down, "re" means "again," and "spect" comes from "to see." So, to re-spect literally means 'to look again.'

That's what I strive to do. In every season, especially the hard ones, I try to look again at His plan. To return to Him. To seek His perspective. To ask, "Father, help me see this the way Thou does."

This is the work of Discipleship: to keep coming back, again and again, not just to understand, but to know more deeply. Sometimes, to be reminded. Sometimes, to see something I missed the first time. And often, to see myself, my circumstances, and my purpose through His Eternal lens.

The more I study the great Plan of Happiness, the more I realize it's not a one-time lesson. It's a lifelong unfolding. The Lord is always ready to give us further light and knowledge, if we are willing to return and look again.

Chapter Seven

— ✦ —

From Stumbling Blocks To Stepping Stones

"The Flood of Information Available at Our Fingertips, Ironically, Makes It Increasingly Difficult to Determine What Is True." - President Russell M. Nelson

Truth, in a world of noise, requires discernment, and discernment requires constant divine connection.

I've worked nearly every year since I was fourteen. I've always needed to pull my weight financially, especially after leaving home for University. That meant a long list of bosses, some wonderful, others deeply challenging. With each new job, I faced a choice: pray to see this child of God the way He sees them and stay, or walk away.

There were times I believed I needed to change, mold myself into the image of my superiors to succeed. But that wasn't always wise.

For a long time, I wrestled with understanding which attributes were truly mine, those that reflected the woman God was shaping me to become. What qualities was I meant to keep and refine under the Spirit's tutelage? And which ones did I need to let go of?

The one that confused me most was meekness.

I used to equate meekness with weakness, quiet, passive, and easily dismissed. It never struck me as something to aspire to. In fact, it felt like the opposite of what I needed to survive or succeed. I couldn't imagine how that trait could possibly fit into the bold, purpose-driven life I felt called to live.

My mindset changed one Sunday in a Gospel Doctrine class.

Someone described meekness in a way I had never heard before. They said, "It's like wielding a great sword. You have the power. You know exactly how to use it. But you choose not to. Meekness isn't about shrinking back, it's about standing tall and strong, and choosing not to be moved by anything that isn't of God."

That hit me.

Meekness isn't powerlessness; it's power under control. It's restraint, not silence. It's courage, anchored in Faith in the Savior, Jesus Christ, in who He is, what He can do, and exercising trust in Him. And from that day on, I stopped resisting the idea of becoming meek and started seeking it instead. I've since learned that there's great wisdom in timing. Not every environment is safe for honest feedback, and not every heart is ready to receive it, including mine.

Whenever I read about the sons of Mosiah burying their weapons of war, I couldn't help but wonder what my own weapon was. The answer came quickly: my tongue.

At times, unkind or impulsive words would spill from my mouth, and I knew they had the power to wound. I also knew that burying this particular weapon, this habit, was something I couldn't do alone. It would take the refining power of Jesus Christ.

His grace is sufficient for you, and when paired with your willing sacrifice, the Holy Ghost reveals powerful Principles and Doctrines that sharpen your spiritual discernment, making it easier to choose between right and wrong with clarity and confidence.

So I began to strive. I repented often. I studied the scriptures and prayed for help. Again and again, I brought this weakness to the Lord. And slowly, sometimes painfully, I began to change.

I've learned how to hold my tongue. How to pause before speaking. How to choose grace over reaction.

It's still a daily effort. Each morning offers a fresh chance to try again. But I've come to believe that even the smallest attempts to lay down our personal weapons of war, especially with the Savior's help, are counted by Heaven as acts of great faith.

In the book of Alma, we read that the Anti-Nephi-Lehies didn't just set their swords aside; they buried them. The scripture records:

"We will hide away our swords, yea, even we will bury them deep in the earth, that they may be kept bright, as a testimony that we have never used them, at the last day."

There's something deeply intentional about that choice. When you simply lay something down, it's easy to reach for it again, especially when life gets hard or when old habits resurface without thought. But burying it? That's different. To bury something deep is an intentional act of surrender, a way of creating distance from what you've already decided no longer belongs in your life.

Elder D. Todd Christofferson taught:

"Burying our weapons of rebellion against God simply means yielding to the enticing of the Holy Spirit, putting off the natural man, and becoming 'a saint through the Atonement of Christ the Lord.' It means putting the first commandment first in our lives. It means letting God prevail."

That kind of submission takes humility. It takes spiritual help from the only Power to help change behavior. And it requires us to embrace the hit of our own shortcomings, not because it's easy or pleasant, but because it's essential.

It's only when we choose to lay our weapons to rest, burying them deep, beyond easy reach, that we create space for the healing and transformative Priesthood Power of God to enter in.

"Priesthood is the power and Authority that God gives to man to act in all things necessary for the Salvation of God's children. The blessings of the Priesthood are available to all who receive the Gospel."

It is through His Priesthood Power, extended to His children on earth, that real change begins. And in that sacred transformation, we discover peace, strength, and divine purpose.

"There is a difference between the Authority of the Priesthood and the Power of the Priesthood. Priesthood Authority comes through ordination to the Priesthood or through Church callings and assignments given by Church leaders who hold Priesthood keys. Power comes from personal righteousness."

Learning what meekness truly is, and just as importantly, what it is not, opened my heart to a deeper understanding of the Priesthood Power of God. Every time I sincerely seek to change, to lay aside parts of the natural man, the Lord not only shows me how to do it, He blesses me with revelation that strengthens my Testimony of His love. A love so personal, so intentional, it reminds me that He knows exactly where I am, what I need, and who I am becoming.

But like any child learning what they should do, I sometimes fell short. I forgot. I misstepped. And those moments often led to another round of uncomfortable, but necessary, lessons.

I sometimes find myself throwing up my hands and saying, "That's not fair!" whether it's due to being overworked, misunderstood, or on the receiving end of what I perceive as harsh or unjust feedback.

Until I learned: "Fair is a place where pigs win ribbons. It's not a place for me."

So what do you do when life seems unfair?

You don't make a list of everything that's wrong and stew in it like ingredients simmering in a self-pity stew. You don't turn up the heat until you boil over with resentment and start whaling, 'wo is me." You steady your thoughts because distraction can lead to destruction. When I find myself swimming in negative self-talk, I try to seek out the voices that speak light, voices that point me back to truth. Elder Dale G. Renlund helped me realize it's not about what is "fair," it's about who I trust in when life feels challenging,

"Nothing compares to the unfairness He endured. ... But He chose to do so because of His love for us and for Heavenly Father. Salvation is a gift we don't deserve and cannot earn. But the Savior offers it to all if we choose to turn to Him."

And He continues:

"In the eternities, Heavenly Father and Jesus Christ will resolve all unfairness. Because of Him, we can have peace in this world and be of good cheer. If we let Him, Jesus Christ will consecrate unfairness for our gain... He will not just console us and restore what was lost; He will use the unfairness for our benefit."

I have felt the truth of that promise in my own life. The Savior hasn't always removed the struggle, but He has repurposed the pain. He has taken the most unfair, unexplainable moments and gently transformed them into experiences that refined me, taught me, and deepened my trust in Him.

It's not about fairness. It's about faith. And who I choose to follow when the path feels heavy.

There have been seasons when my workplace felt like a battlefield, when bosses were unreasonable, or feedback stung, or I found myself misunderstood. And yet, every time I took that to the Lord, He either softened the other person's heart or softened mine. Some of the colleagues I once struggled with are now dear friends, because Christ removed the stumbling blocks that kept me from seeing them as He sees them. How did it happen? I prayed, often and intentionally, to feel genuine love for that individual.

When someone asked President Nelson if being a Prophet was difficult, he responded joyfully, "Of course it's hard!" Not as a complaint, but as a declaration. The Prophet of the Lord gladly rejoices in this work. Then he added, "Everything to do with becoming more like the Savior is difficult."

That truth has shaped the way I see opposition. Through faith in my divine relationship with Heavenly Father, and remembering that Jesus Christ is not just my Redeemer, but also my elder Brother, I've learned to see stumbling blocks as sacred opportunities. Stepping stones that pave the way to my eternal home.

We may feel like we're walking from one obstacle to another, wondering if things will ever improve. And when setbacks come, especially when they follow effort, obedience, or faith, it can feel like failure. Like, we just don't have what it takes.

I've been there. Loss of income when you aren't financially stable or have reserves, when a prayer you have been fasting for is taking longer than you'd hoped. Walked into a meeting or a gathering confident and leaving deflated. Hitting all your benchmarks, only to be overlooked for a promotion or bonus. I've been told to smile and nod at feedback I wasn't allowed to explain. Those moments can gut your motivation. Leave you angry, even bitter.

But when a dream is in your hands, and the world knocks it to the floor, how you respond will shape your becoming.

I've lived those shattered moments more than once. And I'm certain there will be more to come. But I've also learned that the only power strong enough to lift me above those feelings is Jesus Christ.

President Nelson taught:

"Faith in Jesus Christ is the greatest power available in this life. Faith is the power that enables the unlikely to accomplish the impossible. With faith in Jesus Christ, God's children can move mountains in their lives."

I look back at the doors slammed shut, the opportunities yanked away, the false accusations that cornered me, and I realize now: those moments chipped away at parts of me that couldn't stay. Not to destroy me. But to remake me. Not until I was nothing... but until I was different in Him. Elder Jeffrey R. Holland once said:

"Faith is to agree unconditionally, and in advance, to whatever conditions God may require in both the near and distant future."

It became a turning point in my Discipleship.

For a time, I wrestled with the idea of faith when the miracle didn't come. How do I have faith in something that might not happen? If miracles are subject to God's will, then what good is my faith?

I was thinking about it all wrong.

Faith precedes the miracle. And more importantly, faith isn't in the outcome, it's in Christ.

When the miracle I prayed for didn't come, I started to see the miracles that did: peace in my heart, promptings from the Spirit, joy that couldn't be explained.

President Nelson said it beautifully:

"The mountains in our lives do not always move how or when we would like. But our faith will always propel us forward. Faith always increases our access to Godly power.

The Savior is never closer to you than when you are facing or climbing a mountain with faith."

We often hear stories of miracles after the trial of faith, the healing, the reunion, the breakthrough, the protection. And those are real. The Lord is absolutely capable of working wonders.

But there is a miracle we often overlook: the miracle of faith itself.

Faith is a gift. It's a miracle that grows quietly in the hearts of those who believe when there's no evidence to believe. If you're exercising faith right now, if you're still praying, still trying, still trusting, you are already witnessing a miracle.

So when your mind races toward a miraculous outcome, pause. Refocus your gaze. Let the faith you're practicing right now be enough. Let it be beautiful. Let it satisfy your soul.

True success isn't measured by the absence of setbacks, but by the way you rise after them. Grace doesn't always appear as a glimpse of your future; it reveals itself in hindsight. Look back at the road you have traveled, at the challenges you have endured, and you will see it woven into every step. Even the simple gift of reflection is evidence of grace at work.

C.S. Lewis wrote:

"God allows us to experience the low points of life in order to teach us lessons that we could learn in no other way."

And President Nelson gave us this charge:

"Take intentional steps to grow in your confidence before the Lord."

That is what I am learning to do. Step by step, hit by hit, miracle by miracle.

Transitioning from a workaholic to a mother felt like an anvil had dropped on my head, a hit I was utterly unprepared for. No one teaches you how to unlearn the Type A habits that once made you successful: the structure, the control, the constant productivity. Suddenly, I was thrust into a world of complete unpredictability, where schedules were shattered by nap refusals and mood swings replaced Key Performance Indicators. And I had to relearn how to live, lead, and love in a space where nothing went according to plan.

A Stake President once taught me: there's a difference between freedom and Agency. Freedom can be taken away, negotiated, or restricted. But Agency, our God-given power to choose, is eternal. No one can take away our ability to choose faith, to follow Jesus Christ, and to trust in His promises. Embracing that truth, and the responsibility that comes with it, has shaped the way I navigate this ever-unfolding forest of motherhood. I want to do this work, and I desire to do it with gladness.

After experiencing the heartbreak of a miscarriage, my husband and I were blessed with a beautiful baby girl almost one year later. We had no idea what we were doing. But even through the fog of sleepless nights and the chaos of learning everything for the first time, there was this quiet, sustaining happiness. No, we weren't "prepared" in the worldly sense for this sacred calling. But God had been molding us long before she ever arrived -into the parents she needed right now.

Who you are, with all your shortcomings and struggles, is precisely who the Lord knew your children would need. They were entrusted to you not so they could watch perfection, but so they could witness discipleship. What blesses them most is not a flawless parent, but a faithful one—someone who strives, who loves, who repents, who forgives, and who rises again and again.

When your heart is turned toward righteousness, Christ sanctifies even what you may see as failure. He molds weakness into wisdom, sorrow into strength, and trial into testimony. In His hands, your efforts, however imperfect, become holy instruments, shaping both you and your child in His Covenant care.

And we're still learning that she, and later her younger brother, are molding us into who we told God we'd become.

I used to daydream about motherhood, how I'd glide gracefully from task to task, balancing babies on my hip while serving up warm meals and checking in on neighbors. I'd envisioned a spotless home, a well-dressed family, time carved out for passion projects, daily workouts, and maybe a weekly lunch with friends. I suppose I had watched one too many Julie Andrews movies.

Then reality arrived, wrapped in swaddles, tears, teething rings, and holy exhaustion. One afternoon, I found myself curled up on the pantry floor, eating cookie butter straight from the jar, praying that my daughter's 34-minute nap would somehow stretch to 40. (Spoiler: it didn't.) I was physically spent, emotionally raw, and completely unsure of who I was becoming.

And that's when I read the quote, one that broke me open and stitched me back together all at once. Attributed to Marjorie Pay Hinckley but actually shared by Nadine Miner Hobby:

"I don't want to drive up to the pearly gates in a shiny sports car, wearing beautifully tailored clothes, my hair expertly coiffed, and with long, perfectly manicured fingernails. I want to drive up in a station wagon that has mud on the wheels from taking kids to scout camp. I want to be there with a smudge of peanut butter on my shirt from making sandwiches for a sick neighbor's children. I want to be there with a little dirt under my fingernails from helping to weed someone's garden. I want to be there with children's sticky kisses on my cheeks and the tears of a friend on my shoulder. I want the Lord to know I was really here, and that I really lived."

Tears streamed down my cheeks. Something in me softened. I began to shed the skin of what I thought motherhood should look like. I stopped clinging to expectations and started embracing the real, raw beauty of what was right in front of me.

I changed my language, replacing "I have to" with "I get to."

I stopped measuring success by the condition of my floors and started focusing on the feeling in our home.

I let go of perfect and reached for presence.

And slowly, something changed. Not overnight. Not all at once. But purposefully, through grace and grit and practice. I began to see the sacredness in the ordinary. In diaper changes and dishes. In late-night rocking sessions and early-morning tantrums. In my unofficial role as a stain-removal specialist. On the hardest days, I'd hum to myself, "This is my sacred duty," a quiet anthem to keep joy near.

Strength is measured in persistence. Grace is the quiet evidence that you were never alone.

Above the door in our home hangs a piece of wood with a phrase etched into it:

"We live after the manner of happiness."

It's a daily reminder that happiness is not a condition of circumstance, it's a choice. No one else can give it to me. I have to choose it. In the mess. In the miracles. In the middle of it all.

And when chaos calls, as it often does, I simply say, "You're welcome here, as long as you bring your sister, Charity."

President Spencer W. Kimball once said, "We have motive power and are therefore able... to move ourselves as we want to go." And I believe that's the power of Agency. To choose gratitude. To choose growth. To choose grace over guilt.

One more truth that's taken root in my heart over the years:

Worthiness is not flawlessness.

God loves us not after we've figured it out, but as we're learning. He doesn't wait for perfection. He meets us where we are, in my case, in the pantry. In the prayers. In the late nights and the long days. His love is constant, and His patience is infinite.

And I'm learning, day by day, to love myself the way He loves me. Mess and all.

Chapter Eight

— ✦ —

I Need You. To Do More.

"If Ye Will Awake and Arouse Your Faculties, even to an Experiment Upon My Words, And Exercise a Particle of Faith... Let This Desire Work in You, Even Until Ye Believe..." -Alma 32:37

There was a season of my life, before I was married, while living in New York, when the word overwhelmed barely scratched the surface of what I was experiencing. I was juggling too many things, most of them good, but I felt buried beneath the weight of it all. Something inside me knew: this can't be what the Lord intended.

So I dropped to my knees, right there on the floor of my bedroom, and began to pray. I poured out my heart, desperate for relief. "What should I do? How can I stop feeling like this?"

And then, as clearly as if someone had whispered it in my ear, I heard:

"I need you to do more."

I collapsed onto the rug in disbelief, face down, sobbing. That couldn't be right. I was already exhausted, emotionally, spiritually, and physically. Do more? Surely I had misunderstood. I sat back up, wiped my tears on my sleeve, and tried again, like shaking a spiritual Magic 8-Ball, hoping for a different answer.

Again, it came:

"I need you to do more."

This time I said it out loud, half shouting, half pleading, "I can't do more! I'm exhausted!"

I didn't reject the answer, but I also didn't understand it. A week passed. Then a month. I had somewhat forgotten about that moment, but it lingered like a quiet echo in the back of my mind.

Eventually, while studying my scriptures, the words returned: "I need you to do more."

Still confused, but ready to listen, I knelt again, this time asking for understanding, not escape.

Silence.

Frustrated, but not faithless, I returned to my scripture study. Weeks passed. Then months. Still no clarity.

So I did the only thing I could: I kept doing what I was already doing, but with a better attitude. I prayed for more joy, for a lighter heart, for the ability to focus on the light I could see instead of the answers I didn't yet have.

And over time, the burden began to lift, not because the tasks lessened, but because I had changed.

Nearly a year later, I remembered that prayer. I returned to my knees, but this time with peace in my heart. I thanked the Lord for lightening my load, and I repented for the doubt I had allowed to creep in.

Then, gently, I asked again: "What did You mean by 'I need you to do more?'"

The answer came, not as a new phrase, but as a punctuation shift.

In my mind's eye, I saw it clearly:

"I need you. To do more."

Tears filled my eyes as the Spirit wrapped around me. The Lord hadn't been asking for more tasks; He was inviting me into partnership. He was saying, "I need you. I love you. I want you to be part of My work."

The second part, "To do more," wasn't a demand. It was a divine invitation.

"I want to use you. Will you let Me do more with your life?"

He wasn't asking me to do more on my own. He was asking me to let Him magnify what I was already doing. To trust Him with my capacity. To let Him prevail.

Elder Jeffrey R. Holland once said:

"Man's extremity is God's opportunity... If we will be humble and faithful, if we will be believing and not curse God for our problems, He can turn the unfair and inhumane and debilitating prisons of our lives into Temples, or at least into circumstances that bring comfort, revelation, divine companionship, and peace."

While reading an article in LDS Living by Heidi A. Smith, I gained a deeper understanding of what Heavenly Father was showing me about this moment. She wrote, "When we seek God in His house, the holy Temple of the

Lord, His perfect, eternal order can bring about the highest order within us, transforming us in unparalleled ways."

To illustrate this truth, she used the example of weight training. A lifter doesn't grow stronger by keeping the weights light forever. Real growth requires resistance. That's why lifters use a spotter, someone who steps in just enough to keep the lift safe, but not so much that the lifter is robbed of the struggle that builds strength.

Our spiritual growth works the same way. God is the perfect spotter. He knows exactly when to ease our burdens and when to let us strain beneath the weight, because it's in that very struggle that our spiritual muscles form. In the beginning, when our faith is new and tender, He carries more of the load. But as we step into the Temple and Covenant with Him, we take on higher laws, and with them, greater responsibility. He doesn't increase the weight to overwhelm us, but to shape us into who we were always meant to become.

And here's the miracle: as the weight increases, so does our access to divine strength. Temple Covenants bind us to Christ in a way nothing else can. Yes, prayer, scripture study, and service sustain us. But it is in the Temple that we are anchored to a power strong enough not only to slow the pull of spiritual entropy, but to overcome it entirely.

What you couldn't know while reading this book is what's happening in my life as I write these very words.

From the outside, we may look like a thriving young family of four, two children under three. But behind the curtain?

My husband was let go from his job just a month ago when the company's funding fell through. I, too, am unemployed. And in the month my son was born, my former employer served me with a lawsuit, legal fees now stretching beyond what we ever thought we'd have to carry.

We're struggling to pay our mortgage. We're relying on help from my in-laws. Two of my immediate family members are enduring serious health battles, one with mental illness, another with a debilitating medical condition. And yet, somehow, I am filled with joy.

Yes, joy.

Because in the middle of this hardship, God gave me time with my husband and children, sweet, uninterrupted time before our daughter starts school. Time to write this book. Time to reflect. Time to testify.

It has taken me ten years to finish Embrace the Hit, and now I understand why. I needed this chapter of my life to be part of it. Without it, I would've missed the miracle that I am currently receiving by reviewing old journal entries and highlighted quotes.

For years, this book felt like an unfulfilled assignment hanging over me. I even began to feel guilt and shame for not finishing it sooner. But guilt and shame? They're not of God. They are tools of the adversary, designed to paralyze. All good things are from God, and He has always known the perfect time.

Had I finished this book when I first felt prompted, I wouldn't have had this Testimony. I wouldn't have witnessed firsthand the unfolding of miracles amidst the chaos of my entangled life. I wouldn't have been able to say, with full conviction, that He is a God of right now, a God of perfect timing and relentless love.

If my life had gone the way I planned, I may have missed the happiness He had in store for me.

Finishing this book feels like completing a sacred errand. I've witnessed the windows of Heaven open over my family, not because everything was removed or fixed, but because God is near.

There are blessings in this chaos I can't even begin to put into words.

So if the Lord has placed something on your heart, a calling, a project, a prompting, begin. And if it takes time, let it. He may not ask you to finish it right now. But as you walk with Him, He'll shape you through the process.

Let Him weave His divine hand into your life so that His glory, not just your effort, shines through you.

We are living in the days leading up to the Second Coming of Jesus Christ. The Lord is hastening His work. And He wants you, not just your time or your checklist, but your heart, your faith, and your unique contribution.

He delights in you.

And He needs you.

To do more.

This quote was said to the women of the church by President Russell M. Nelson

"We need women who are organized and women who can organize. We need women with executive ability who can plan and direct and administer; women who can teach, women who can speak out. ...

We need women with the gift of discernment who can view the trends in the world and detect those that, however popular, are shallow or dangerous."

He continues, "Today, let me add that we need women who know how to make important things happen by their faith and who are courageous defenders of morality and families in a sin-sick world. We need women who are devoted to shepherding God's children along the Covenant Path toward Exaltation; women who know how to receive personal Revelation, who understand the power and peace of the Temple Endowment; women who know how to call upon the powers of Heaven to protect and strengthen children and families; women who teach fearlessly."

He confirmed, "We need women who have a bedrock understanding of the Doctrine of Christ and who will use that understanding to teach and help raise a sin-resistant generation. We need women who can detect deception in all of its forms. We need women who know how to access the power that God makes available to Covenant keepers and who express their beliefs with confidence and charity. We need women who have the courage and vision of our Mother Eve.

My dear sisters, nothing is more crucial to your Eternal life than your own conversion. It is converted, Covenant-keeping women, women like my dear wife Wendy, whose righteous lives will increasingly stand out in a deteriorating world and who will thus be seen as different and distinct in the happiest of ways."

When I think about the unique influence each individual carries, their personal sphere, their voice, their Testimony of Jesus Christ, and Heavenly Father's Plan, I feel excitement. There is power in people who embrace challenges and opposition without absorbing the world's negative interpretations of them. As we stand in truth and testify of Him, we become part of something far greater. We help usher in the Second Coming of our Savior.

I've come to understand that one of the great purposes of this life is to choose, daily, deliberately, whether we want to belong to the Kingdom of God more than we want anything else. That choice shows up in the smallest decisions: Will I be entertained, or will I be engaged?

And I'll be honest, I truly hope I'm not caught binge-watching a TV series when the Savior returns.

It takes effort and intention to live engaged. I have to actively seek the Lord's help to stay focused on what matters most, to choose meaningful work, spiritual nourishment, and the kind of Discipleship that prepares me to stand ready when He comes.

We touched on this earlier, but I want to dive into it a bit more. When President Russell M. Nelson, Prophet, Seer, and Revelator, was asked, "Is it hard to be a Prophet? Are you, like, really busy?" his response was immediate and filled with joy:

"Of course it's hard! Everything to do with becoming more like the Savior is difficult. The Lord loves effort because effort brings rewards that can't come without it. It takes effort, a lot of hard work, a lot of study, and there's never an end. That's good! That's good because we're always progressing. Even in the next life, we're making progress."

I often ask myself, what would shift in my heart if I replaced the word "Prophet" with "Daughter of God"?

"Is it hard to be a Daughter of God? Are you, like, really busy?"

The answer would likely be the same. Of course, it's hard. Everything about becoming like the Savior requires effort, joyful, stretching, refining effort.

As I pondered how to have the spiritual gift of joy, I had to return to the beginning. What is joy?

Joy is not just a fleeting feeling. Joy is Him. It is everything Jesus Christ is, everything He represents, and everything He continues to do. It is found in what He has done for us, in the depth of His love, in the truths He left to guide us back to our Eternal home. Joy is knowing who we are to Him and to our Heavenly Father. His Gospel, His words, and His messengers all lead us back to that truth. And that truth is joy.

But then a question stirred in me: If I know Him, if I follow Him, if I strive to walk in His ways, why don't I always feel joy?

Why do you think President Nelson could answer that question about being a Prophet with such light and enthusiasm, even while acknowledging it is hard? He shows us that hard work and effort don't cancel joy. The pioneers, the early Saints, did they have easy lives? Not at all. And yet, they sang, rejoiced, and bore their burdens with joy.

So what robs us of joy?

The Spirit taught me: the absence of joy comes from forgetting.

The Book of Mormon uses the word remember 220 times, making it one of the most repeated words in the text. Think of that! This book, described as the most correct book on earth, written for our day, places incredible emphasis on remembering.

For me, joy slips when I stop remembering Him.

This was hard to face. I love Him. I want His Spirit with me always. But the "daily grind" can distract me. Even when I'm busy with good things, serving my family, fulfilling responsibilities, if my mind drifts from Him, I can quickly become overwhelmed, stressed, or weary.

Sometimes, when I'm drained, I turn to distractions, like binge-watching shows, just to numb myself from what's weighing me down. Breaks are fine, even needed, but I've had to ask: Do these breaks fill me up, or do they leave me numb?

We are reminded so often to remember Him because when we remember who He is and who we are to Him, joy flows back in. When I realize I'm not feeling joy, I try not to focus on the word forgot, because that feels heavy. Instead, I see it as an invitation:

An Aha-moment- here's another chance to remember Him again.

If we ever become too busy for the Lord, there's a good chance we're more busy than the Lord ever intended us to be.

One of my favorite scriptures is 3 Nephi 13:22:

"The light of the body is the eye; if therefore thine eye be single, thy whole body shall be full of light."

When we fix our gaze on the Savior, when we remember Him, we become filled with His light. We begin to see every ordinary moment as a sacred chance to reconnect. The Holy Ghost never tires of offering those opportunities, just as the adversary never tires of distracting us. But here's the thing: three stand with us, our Heavenly

Father, Jesus Christ, and the Holy Ghost. That's three against one. And that's a battle we can win.

To find joy in the daily grind, we need the contrast. We need the moments that challenge us so that we can recognize the sweetness of joy when it comes. In those hard moments, let us remember Him. Let us rejoice in what He has already done; our Salvation is purchased. Before we even came to earth, we chose His side. His love, His forgiveness, and His joy are unshakable.

Pray to see the moments where joy is waiting for you. Pray to remember Him.

As Lehi said in his vision in 1 Nephi 8:12:

"And as I partook of the fruit thereof, it filled my soul with exceedingly great joy; wherefore, I began to be desirous that my family should partake of it also, for I knew that it was desirable above all other fruit."

Joy is Him. And the absence of joy is simply the absence of remembering Him.

So let us go to our knees in every opportunity to remember. Let us rejoice in what He has done, who we are, and the Plan of Happiness we are living right now. And when we remember Him, let us linger a little longer, like Enoch, allowing that joy to deepen.

Then, filled with His light, let us share it. Share Him. Help others see their own moments of remembrance because I know that when we remember Him, the Creator, our Advocate, the Bread of Life, we will find joy.

Joy in that simple, powerful act of remembering Jesus Christ. By so doing, you will remember who you are, to whom you are connected, and your divine heritage.

Chapter Nine

— ✦ —

Embrace Your Influence

"Influence Is Usually Something We Don't Consciously Exert. In Fact, We May Not Even Want to Exert It. But It Is There. Whether for Good or Bad, Whether Welcomed or Shunned, Influence Is Something Everyone Exerts Upon Those Around Him." -Dr. Lindsay R. Curtis

In a world obsessed with followers, likes, and "going viral," it's easy to believe influence is something you earn or build. But spiritual influence begins not with numbers, but with choices. It starts the moment you decide to follow Jesus Christ and embrace the hits (good and bad) of this life with Him.

I want you to take a moment to reflect:

What does the word influence mean to you?

Who do you consider to be influential?

What makes them so?

Now, can you see any of those same qualities in yourself?

Most people I speak to don't immediately recognize their own influence. Some downplay it, saying they only influence their kids or coworkers, or that they're in a season where their reach feels small. But I want you to know something: God doesn't measure influence by audience size. He measures it by intent, by effort, by love. If you are on this earth, you are influencing someone. Period.

I didn't always see myself this way either.

And yet, when asked to speak to a youth group about "influence," I felt self-conscious. Surely there were others more qualified. But it struck me, why did people think I had influence? Was it because I was in 100 million homes on television? Hadn't I been influencing people long before anyone knew my name?

The world teaches that influence is external, earned, or performed. The Lord teaches that influence is quiet, internal, and sacred. Christ like influence flows through persuasion, long-suffering, gentleness, meekness, and love unfeigned (see D&C 121:41-42).

True influence is acting in a way that assists someone's understanding of what it means to follow Jesus Christ. And it can happen in a Temple, in a grocery store, or at the dinner table. Your daily choices, how you respond to stress, how you treat others, how you live your Covenants, those choices preach louder than any microphone ever could.

Influence begins with Agency.

"There is one, above all others, whose personal influence covers the continents, spans the oceans, and penetrates the hearts of true believers. He Atoned for the sins of mankind. He is a Teacher of truth, but He is more than a Teacher. He is the Exemplar of the perfect life- but He is more than an exemplar. He is the Great Physician- but He is more than a Physician. He is the literal Savior of the world, the Son of God, the Prince of Peace, the Holy One of Israel, even the risen Lord."

Agency is your divine ability to choose. It's your decision how you show up each day and decide who you will be.

Spencer W. Kimball taught, "We had Agency then [in the pre-existence], and we chose to come to Earth though we knew there would be hazards and hard things. We had sufficient confidence then to follow the plan of Jesus Christ."

That same Agency empowers us today to be Disciples, Ambassadors of the Lord.

You may not feel like a leader in the world's eyes, but if you are following Christ, you are leading in the Lord's way. Whether you're mothering one child, mentoring a friend, or quietly living a Christ-centered life, you are influencing hearts.

You don't need a platform, a title, or a spotlight to have influence. What you need is a willing heart.

I invite you to pause and ask a simple but powerful question:

"Heavenly Father, who did You create me to be? Help me see my influence through Your eyes."

President David O. McKay once taught,

"There is one responsibility that no one can evade. That is the effect of one's personal influence."

Whether or not the world recognizes your influence, the Heavens already do. And as you remember who you are - a child of God, who you follow - Jesus Christ, you will begin to uncover the quiet, radiant power of righteous influence within you.

This is Understanding the Responsibility of Personal Influence.

This isn't about traditional leadership or social media status. It's not about how many people follow you. It's about discovering that you already carry influence, divinely appointed influence, and learning how to use it with intention, humility, and courage.

You have influence, whether you believe it or not. And when you begin to understand Agency as the root of that influence, you can start making choices that align with the Savior and reflect His light into the lives of others.

Your Testimony matters.

You do not need a flawless résumé, a polished background, or the perfect words. What you do need is a Testimony, simple, sincere, and born of experience. The Holy Ghost, one of the original influencers, teaches us how to bear witness in ways that are natural, authentic, and powerful.

There has been inspired counsel given to Latter-day Saints about what to do with our influence when we choose to follow Jesus Christ.

Elder Jeffrey R. Holland once taught:

"Our duty now is to 'invite all to come unto Christ.' We cannot be satisfied receiving spiritual blessings for ourselves; we must lead the people we love to those same blessings, and as Disciples of Jesus Christ, we must love everyone. The Savior's charge to Peter is also a charge to us: 'When thou art converted, strengthen thy brethren.'"

Your influence grows every time you feast on the Word of God.

It multiplies when you use your Agency to align with the Spirit. The Lord Himself promises this:

In Doctrine and Covenants 76:5 6, it states, "I, the Lord, am merciful and gracious unto those who fear me, and delight to honor those who serve me in righteousness and in truth unto the end. Great shall be their reward, and eternal shall be their glory."

As you study the Savior's life, you'll notice something remarkable: He always focused on the one. And yet, through that Holy pattern, billions have been, and continue to be, influenced.

Elder David A. Bednar put it this way:

"Jesus then becomes much more than the central character in Scripture stories; His example and teachings influence our every desire, thought, and action."

In today's world, the righteous influence of a family can often feel unpopular or even attacked. But the truth remains: that kind of influence ripples through generations and into eternity.

And to withstand the pull of worldly influence, we must learn to heed not the voices that try to diminish our worth or distract us from our Divine purpose. This can only happen with the help of the Holy Ghost, a companion we cannot afford to live without.

President Russell M. Nelson has pleaded with us to seek that companionship daily. Elder Bednar affirmed:

"Our covenant connection with God and Jesus Christ is the channel through which we can receive the capacity and strength to 'heed not.' And this bond is strengthened as we continually hold fast to the rod of iron. Please note that the ability to resist the temptations and the fiery darts of the adversary is promised to those individuals who 'hold fast to' rather than merely 'cling to' the word of God."

So again, I ask:

Who did God create you to be?

Let Him show you. And then go forward and share your Testimony, your story, your miracles, because the world doesn't need more noise. It needs more light.

And your light, however subtle it may feel, matters. Do not hide it under a bushel. Embrace the hit with Jesus Christ.

Works Cited

Bednar, David A. "But We Heeded Them Not." General Conference, April 2022. The Church of Jesus Christ of Latter-day Saints.

The Book of Mormon: Another Testament of Jesus Christ. Salt Lake City: The Church of Jesus Christ of Latter-day Saints, 1981.

The Book of Mormon. Alma 23–24.

The Book of Mormon. Alma 32:37.

The Book of Mormon. Jacob 7:3.

The Book of Mormon. Ether 12:27.

The Holy Bible: King James Version. Matthew 7:20. Salt Lake City: The Church of Jesus Christ of Latter-day Saints, 1979.

Curtis, Lindsay R. "Everyone Has Influence." Ensign, September 1990.

Doctrine and Covenants 10:43.

Doctrine and Covenants 76:5–6.

Doctrine and Covenants 109:24–28.

Doctrine and Covenants 121:41–42.

Doctrine and Covenants 88:32.

Holland, Jeffrey R. "When Thou Art Converted, Strengthen Thy Brethren." General Conference, April 2004. The Church of Jesus Christ of Latter-day Saints.

Kimball, Spencer W. "The Importance of Personal Influence." Improvement Era, November 1969.

Maxwell, Neal A. "Swallowed Up in the Will of the Father." General Conference, April 1995. The Church of Jesus Christ of Latter-day Saints.

McKay, David O. Gospel Ideals: Selections from the Discourses of David O. McKay. Salt Lake City: Deseret Book, 1953.

Nelson, Russell M. "A Plea to My Sisters." General Conference, October 2015. The Church of Jesus Christ of Latter-day Saints.

Nelson, Russell M. "Revelation for the Church, Revelation for Our Lives." General Conference, April 2018. The Church of Jesus Christ of Latter-day Saints.

Nelson, Russell M. "The Love and Laws of God." Address at Brigham Young University, September 17, 2019.

Packer, Boyd K. "The Study of the Doctrines of the Gospel Will Improve Behavior." Address, 1986. The Church of Jesus Christ of Latter-day Saints.

Smith, Brigham Young. Quoted in Deseret News, April 10, 1861, 41.

Smith, Heidi A. "When We Seek God in His House." LDS Living. Accessed 2023.

Monson, Thomas S. "Your Personal Influence." General Conference, April 2004. The Church of Jesus Christ of Latter-day Saints.

Index

— ✦ —

About The Author

Courtney Spencer was born in South Dakota and raised in Houston, Texas. A graduate of Baylor University, she has been a competitive athlete since the age of three, excelling in gymnastics, track and field, cheerleading, collegiate lacrosse, and later training for the Winter Olympic sport of Skeleton.

At age twenty-six, while living in New York City, Courtney was baptized as a member of The Church of Jesus Christ of Latter-day Saints, an experience that reshaped the course of her life. She is a wife, a mother, an entrepreneur, a speaker, and a former QVC Program Host. Along the way, she has even had the unique opportunity to perform with Beyoncé and Lady Gaga.

Her church service has included roles as a Relief Society teacher, Gospel Doctrine teacher, ward missionary, counselor in both the Relief Society and Primary presidencies, Young Women's President, and counselor in a Stake Young Women presidency. She has also shared her faith and experiences as a presenter at BYU Education Week.

www.ingramcontent.com/pod-product-compliance
Lightning Source LLC
Chambersburg PA
CBHW030845090426
42737CB00009B/1117

9 7 9 8 9 9 3 0 7 7 1 1 6